T0157904

"Reality at its finest! *Supermom* helps readers understand what the reality can be of someone who appears to have everything perfectly together. Everyone should read this book!"

—Crystal Clancy,
Licensed Marriage and Family Therapist

"As a physician, friend, and mother, this book has truly enlightened me. Despite our best attempts at screening new mothers, so many women fall under the radar because their symptoms don't meet the criteria for postpartum depression. Ackerman's candid approach to her experiences with postpartum anxiety lends a voice to the countless women have suffered in silence."

—Regina Cho, MD, FACOG,
Obstetrician and Gynecologist

SUPERMOM

A Postpartum Anxiety Survival Story

Stacey Ackerman

iUniverse, Inc.
Bloomington

Supermom
A Postpartum Anxiety Survival Story

iUniverse books may be ordered through booksellers or by contacting:

iUniverse
1663 Liberty Drive
Bloomington, IN 47403
www.iuniverse.com
1-800-Authors (1-800-288-4677)

ISBN: 978-1-4620-0862-9 (pbk)
ISBN: 978-1-4620-0863-6 (clth)
ISBN: 978-1-4620-0864-3 (ebk)

Library of Congress Control Number: 2011905251

Printed in the United States of America

iUniverse rev. date: 4/19/11

That which does
not kill us makes us
stronger.
—Friedrich Nietzsche

Contents

Preface

I'm really just an ordinary mom. There has never been anything that extraordinary about my life. I'm not a face that you would look at and think, "She needs to be committed to a mental institution," and yet I was.

I'm really just like you. I live in the 'burbs. I drive a minivan. I haul my kids to soccer and swimming lessons. I clean up poop and puke. My house is overflowing with plastic toys. It takes me an hour to wipe up the spilled food off the floor every time we eat a meal. And yes, I have used the TV as a babysitter on more than one occasion. I'm definitely not perfect, yet I strive to be everything to everyone.

Before my own postpartum breakdown, I thought that only *crazy* people had mental-health issues. The truth is, your best friend, your neighbor, or even you can experience postpartum mood disorders—ranging from the baby blues to full-blown psychosis. It doesn't matter who you are or what your background is—we are all susceptible.

I'm not trying to scare you, but to be blatantly honest, our mental health is a fragile thing—given the right ingredients of hormones, sleep deprivation, and stress—anyone of us can break.

If you're a *Supermom,* like I always try to be, you are even more susceptible to postpartum anxiety and panic disorder, like I had after the birth of my third child.

So as you read my story, put on your comfy sweats, ignore the kids asking for another drink of water, grab a glass of wine and a super-sized box of tissues, and realize that if you too are experiencing a postpartum mood disorder you are not alone, and you are not crazy.

You may be a *Supermom* if you exhibit any of these symptoms:

- You give birth, and then go shopping the next day.
- You write unrealistic "To Do" lists.
- You volunteer to help in your kid's classroom, even though you have three other things on your calendar at the same time.
- You don't know what would happen if you lost your smart phone.
- You invite 30 kids to your child's birthday party, complete with craft stations, make-your-own cupcakes and other home-made activities, and you don't ask for help from anyone.
- You make sure your kids lead enriched lives, so you sign them up for music class, soccer, swimming lessons and drama camp, all at the same time.
- You go to 10 different stores looking for the perfect Halloween costumes. Better yet, you decide to make them yourself.
- You strive to have a fabulous career, perfectly maintained home and well-rounded children. Then you feel like crap when this unrealistic expectation isn't met.

Emergency Room Report

Stacey Ackerman is a thirty-five-year-old woman who is feeling extremely anxious and having panic attacks. She feels that she cannot cope. She reports racing thoughts and difficulty concentrating and feels unable to take care of her newborn baby and her other two children. She states that she has been unable to sleep for the past three nights. The patient is alert and anxious but appears cooperative. Her speech is somewhat pressured and she has adequate judgment, perhaps slightly limited insight. No obvious hallucinations or delusions. She denies any intent to harm herself or others, but again states that she feels incapable of caring for her children in her current state.

In this picture, which was taken for a modeling job, we look like a mother and daughter blissfully enjoying life. No one could tell that behind this veneer of perfection, I was severely mentally ill.

Acknowledgments

I couldn't have made it through this turbulent time in my life without many wonderful people by my side. It was their strength and support that got me through the darkest days. Without that, I don't know where I would be today.

First, I want to thank my husband, Eirik. Not many men could take care of two toddlers and a newborn, a wife, the house, and a job with the perseverance that he did. He didn't worry about the small stuff but made sure everyone was taken care of, even putting his own health in jeopardy. He is the wonderful man I married eight years ago and more. We have had some really tough times and this was about the toughest, but he always remained calm and focused. I also want to thank my husband for giving me the confidence and time needed to tell my story. He's always believed in me, even when I've failed to believe in myself. He is the rock that keeps this family together. I couldn't imagine this life without him.

I also want to thank my mother-in-law, Sylvia. She really came through for our family when we needed her the most. Staying with our family for three weeks and making sure that the children were okay was the best gift she could ever give us. It was that peace of mind that got me through those long days in the hospital.

To my dad, Sandy, I know that seeing his daughter in a mental health facility was one of the most difficult things he's ever had to face. And now that I'm a parent, I can understand how awful it must be to see your child suffering. I appreciate his taking me on my first passes outside of the hospital and being there during some very difficult days. I know he was extremely worried about me. Thankfully, the worst is behind us.

To my mom, Harriette, I want to thank her for all of the time she spent taking care of the kids. They say it takes a village to raise a family, and it couldn't have been truer in this situation.

To my good friend and obstetrician, Regina, I want to thank her for telling me to go to the hospital to get the help I needed. She saved me when I didn't know where else to turn. I also want to thank her for visiting me almost every day at the hospital. Seeing her familiar face gave me some sense of normalcy, even if it was only for a few minutes.

To my brother, Brian, and sister-in-law, Erin, even though they were across the country, I felt their care and concern. I know they felt helpless not being near, but my knowing they cared meant so much.

To all of my other family members, friends, and neighbors who helped out our family during this tough time, I thank you. From helping with the children to bringing meals, we couldn't have done it without such a great support system.

To my therapist, Crystal, her knowledge and expertise have been invaluable. She taught me to look deeper within myself.

To the wonderful survivors who I've met while writing this book, they are such an inspiration to me by sharing their stories.

To my children Evan, Eithan, and Emily, they are the loves of my life. It was so heartbreaking to be away from them when I was sick. I am so happy to be back in their lives and I hope that I will never have to leave them again.

Introduction

What went wrong after the birth of my daughter Emily that landed me in a mental institution for nearly two weeks? I'm not sure if I'll ever know the real reason.

Like millions of other women who have suffered from postpartum disorders, I thought I was immune to the disease. I never thought a postpartum mood disorder could happen to me, someone who is always so rational. In fact, before I experienced it, I had never even heard of postpartum anxiety disorder.

There is a lot of information out there about postpartum depression (PPD), but when my symptoms didn't meet the PPD criteria, I went undiagnosed until it was almost too late.

I have always thought of myself as a happy-go-lucky kind of person. I felt relatively *normal* after the births of my first two children, so the postpartum anxiety disorder that came after my daughter Emily's birth came as a real nightmare.

Just recently, I learned that there were hints of anxiety with me for most of my adult life, but they were not recognizable to me or anyone around me because they weren't severe or debilitating.

I am writing this book because I want to educate moms-to-be and clinicians on postpartum anxiety disorders, which can be very different than postpartum depression.

During my six-month battle with postpartum anxiety, panic and mild psychosis, I wasn't weepy or sad. I didn't have thoughts of harming my baby. I wasn't feeling blue. I didn't meet any of the criteria that practitioners use to diagnose postpartum depression, and yet I had one of the most serious cases most of them had ever seen.

My good friend and obstetrician, Dr. Regina Cho, said that if I hadn't gotten help when I did, my situation could have been grave. It's horrifying to think that I could have been the next mom to throw her kids off a bridge or commit suicide. Luckily, I found help before my disease progressed that far.

However, finding the help I needed was extremely difficult when I was in the midst of a crisis. I didn't know who to call, who to turn to, or who to trust. I got the runaround several times before I found the help that I needed to heal. It wasn't until I was halfway through my recovery that I was well enough to do my own research and find some excellent resources.

I hope that by reading my story about postpartum anxiety disorder, moms will be aware of the symptoms if it happens to them, and that they will know who to contact in the event of an emergency.

I want to educate doctors, nurses, social workers, psychiatrists, and other medical practitioners that see new moms that postpartum anxiety disorder is a serious disease, and it doesn't always mimic depression.

By telling my story, I hope that postpartum anxiety disorders become as easily recognizable as postpartum depression.

While the weeks and months after my daughter's birth were the most terrifying moments of my life, I feel that it has brought me a purpose. If I can help just one person who suffers from a postpartum anxiety disorder through this book, then what I went through will bring meaning to my life.

In many ways my sickness has made me a stronger and better parent. While it took a long time to recover, I now look at my one-year-old daughter with awe and appreciation and think, *we made it!*

She is truly my miracle child because there was a time when I didn't think I would ever be able to raise her.

Several people's names have been changed in this story to protect their privacy.

CHAPTER 1

The Darkest Days

What should have been the happiest days of my life turned out to be the darkest days. I had always longed for a daughter, and now that I had one I wasn't sure if I'd ever get to raise her.

I hadn't seen my newborn in more than a week, but it felt like a lifetime. As I sat in the windowsill of my hospital room in the behavioral health unit, I looked outside at the world around me. I saw familiar streets, ordinary people going to visit loved ones, cars driving by, even the downtown Minneapolis skyline in the background. These were all familiar sights that I'd seen a million times before, but life from inside these four walls looked very different.

Most of the time I couldn't remember the simplest things—like how to brush my teeth, take a shower, or comb my hair. The outside world seemed foreign now. I had to think about it really hard to even remember that I had a baby. My engorged and infected breasts were the only hint of reality—the reality that I had to abruptly quit nursing. I was in a different place at this time in my life—one that I wasn't sure I'd ever escape.

My psychiatrist labeled me *Supermom*. He said, "The higher up you are, the farther you have to fall." He characterized me as the woman who juggles so many things that I can no longer keep all of the balls in the air. "Sooner or later something's going to tip," he said. I had a hard time believing him at the time, but now I think he was wise beyond his words.

I used to run around and try to be the perfect mother, wife, entrepreneur, employee, daughter, friend, sister, housekeeper, neighbor, event planner—

the list goes on and on. I still do try to be all of those things, although now I'm more aware of my actions.

Well, one day, my *Supermom* cape broke and I could no longer fly. I remember going to a birthday party with my oldest son, Evan. It was for one of his preschool classmates. His mother had meticulously arranged for everyone to sew an owl costume. I couldn't even figure out how to assemble the darn thing. One of the other moms said, "And there goes Jen, pulling out her *Supermom* cape again."

I wanted to be like her. I wanted to have the perfect craft for my kid's party too. I tried to have a really great fifth birthday party for Evan. I rented a huge tiger jumper, but it rained. I had planned for the kids to plant flowers, but none of them were interested.

Nonetheless, the party wasn't up to my *Supermom* expectations. Now I know that nothing can ever live up to those expectations because they're not realistic.

In my quest to be a super-accomplished woman with a ten page to-do list every day, I often forget some important details because my brain runs on overload.

I'm always the mom who forgets to put diapers in the diaper bag, or goes to the zoo without any snacks. And I am always losing my watch, the silver one that I bought on our trip to Switzerland. One day when I was pouring my corn flakes, the watch fell out. Talk about a great cereal prize!

As part of my *Supermom* persona, I like to have everything meticulously planned out, I want to be in control. *Always.* I hate the feeling of not having control. There is nothing that scares me more.

But it seems like there's this strange thing called *life* that seems to get in the way. The stomach flu, a car accident, an asthma attack, bad weather, or postpartum anxiety that shakes up my system.

Why can't these things be scheduled on my smart phone like everything else? I don't deal well with the unexpected.

After my daughter's birth, more and more stressors entered my life and I tried to hold it all together and stay in control, but I lost it. It's hard to admit, but I *totally* lost it. Sometimes I feel like I'll lose it again, but I'm working on that.

When postpartum anxiety/panic/psychosis hit me after having my third child, it was totally unplanned, unexpected, and it shook up my world like nothing else imaginable.

CHAPTER 2

Welcome to Motherhood—and Colic

My journey into motherhood began five years ago when my newborn son Evan let out the loudest shrill I'd ever heard in my life, and that noise didn't go away for four grueling months.

By the second night in the hospital, we begged the nurse to *please* take him back to the nursery so we could catch a little shut-eye. A few hours later, she brought back our screaming little child and told me he must be hungry.

Are you kidding me? I just fed him!

Evan was a handful, even too much for the nursery to handle. That screaming didn't stop for sixteen weeks, three days, and twelve hours. I was sleep deprived beyond belief, felt some baby blues, and really wasn't sure what I had gotten myself into.

I had originally planned to return to work after twelve weeks, but got laid off of my job when I was eight months pregnant. I felt miserable sitting in my brand new beige rocker from Babies 'R' Us trying to calm my screaming hellion.

I must have called my pediatrician seventy-six times a day! When she asked me where I was, I said I was out shopping with the baby. She gave me a huge lecture about how having a baby means you need to stay home to get the baby on a schedule.

Stay home! I can't do that, I thought.

As someone who thrives on a full schedule, staying home just isn't my speed. I like to run around, always living my life with a fully-booked calendar of events.

Staying at home rocking a baby all day felt so confining. I can remember sitting in that rocking chair with one leg hanging over the edge, staring out at the beautiful summer day and sobbing because I felt like I had given up my entire life.

The elementary school bus comes to our corner and all of the moms stand out there waiting for their kids to get on the bus. One morning after sobbing, I put Evan in his crib and ran out and called for help from the other moms.

"My baby won't quit crying," I sobbed to the moms. "What should I do?" I asked frantically.

I attributed my irrational behavior to sleep deprivation and the screaming baby, but only recently have I recognized that there may have been more to my moods than anyone realized at the time.

When Evan was just a few days old, I desperately wanted to take him for a walk in the new stroller. The problem was, I couldn't tell for sure if I had the baby secured properly in the stroller and I went ballistic. I started kicking the stroller and screaming, finally yelling to my husband, "I'm outta here!" I stormed out of the house and left him with the baby.

A few hours later, after some retail therapy, I returned home calm, cool, and collected. Eirik was completely freaked out. "I thought you had left us for good," he said.

"I just went to Kohl's," I said. I found it strange that he would think I would ever leave him and the new baby.

During the first few days home, the baby went forty-eight hours without ever closing his eyes. The screaming *never* stopped.

This wasn't what I had planned. We were going to plant an 'Evan cherry tree' in the backyard to commemorate his birth. We actually found a tree called an Evan at our local garden store.

My husband Eirik had two weeks paternity leave so we thought we'd have this nice family vacation and do a few renovation projects on the side. Why didn't those birthing classes tell us that we were so far off from reality? A friend of Eirik's said that newborns sleep for eighteen hours a day.

Are you kidding me, our baby doesn't sleep for eighteen minutes a day!

When I took Evan to Mommy and Me class, all of the other babies were quietly cooing or sleeping soundly in their car seats or their mom's arms. My little hellion just screamed. And screamed. And screamed.

Why didn't he come with an instruction manual? Isn't there an off switch?

I remember driving around the surrounding farm towns at 3:00 am listening to Mötley Crue over and over again. We also tried putting him on the dryer. We tried relaxing music. We bounced him up and down and twirled him round and round. He still screamed.

Being a new mom was so different than I had expected. My nineteen-year-old coworker had just had a baby, then immediately put on her size two jean shorts.

I was depressed as my flabby belly hung over my elastic waist pants and my breasts looked like two giant watermelons.

Where had the old Stacey gone and would she ever return?

We had taken birthing classes, breastfeeding classes and read every book at Barnes & Noble, but no one could have told me how difficult being a new mom would be. I felt completely robbed of my freedom. I just wanted to go where I wanted when I wanted, and now that was gone. Forever. I was fat, sleep-deprived, and not at all feeling the *joy* of my new bundle of joy.

At four months, I quit nursing and started my baby on soy formula. It seemed to be the magic ticket, because after that the colic stopped.

Once Evan got over his colicky phase, we finally got into the groove of being parents and I started getting used to being home when the baby napped, even though I didn't like it very much.

We watched every milestone in awe—his first bite of rice cereal to taking his first steps. Just like every first child, his every move was captured on camera, video and scrap-booked.

Right after Evan's first birthday, my husband convinced me to try again. He was really close in age to his two younger sisters and wanted that same closeness for our family. Besides, it could take a while. But it didn't. Our second child was conceived instantaneously.

Early into this pregnancy I was an emotional mess. Money was tight and I worried about how we were going to support both kids. Evan was an active toddler, and I didn't know how I was going to handle two under two. I felt really overwhelmed by the pregnancy.

I recall a time when Eirik and Evan were outside with the neighbors laughing and having a great time, and I was lying in bed crying my eyes out. I didn't want to be pregnant and felt resentful of the decision. This feeling lasted for a few months, but I was unaware that this was an illness and never sought out any medical help.

During this pregnancy, I started having difficulty breathing and went to the emergency room where I was diagnosed with pneumonia. I was about sixteen weeks along and asked if they would do an ultrasound just to make sure everything was okay.

We got a sneak peak at the baby and found out it was a boy. While I was happy that the baby was fine, I felt a little disappointed about the gender. I never had a sister and I have always been a girly-girl. I love doing hair and spent many years as a makeup artist. I love to shop and go crazy for baby girl dresses. We already had a girl's name picked out—Audrey Sophia.

Our son Eithan was born on Easter Sunday in 2007. The delivery went smoothly—in fact I never even had to push—he just fell out!

When the epidural wore off I reached over to try and pick him up and realized it was too painful, and I still couldn't feel my legs. I could barely stand and when I tried to walk it hurt so badly that I could only do the granny shuffle.

My obstetrician consulted a neurologist who ordered an MRI. They tried to tell me that I had strained a muscle from pushing, but I snapped back at them, "I didn't even push at all!" I was convinced that the epidural needle had injured a nerve, causing my paralysis.

This temporary paralysis lasted for nearly two weeks and Evan was a very busy twenty-two-month old! I spent the first few weeks home in bed, barely able to pick up my new son. All I wanted to do was get out in the fresh air and go for a walk, but I couldn't. There is nothing I hate more than feeling stuck. But I was stuck. I was helpless. Luckily, my mom stepped in and helped me take care of the kids for a few weeks.

CHAPTER 3

Going for Number Three

While we were really happy with our two boys, the talk of a third child started popping up like tulips in the spring.

Eirik came from a family of three kids, so to him this seemed normal. I grew up with divorced parents and lived with my mom and younger brother, so a family of five seemed *huge* to me.

I had several concerns about having another baby.

Can I handle three small children? Maybe we should just be thankful for what we have.

"If we don't try you'll never have a girl," Eirik said.

"Yeah, but what if we have three boys?" I replied. "Then I'll really be outnumbered!"

"We won't, it's going to be a girl next time," he said with complete confidence.

Normally I would not believe someone who told me this, but he was two for two so far. While he doesn't like to admit it, my husband has an incredible sixth sense. The moment that Evan was conceived he said he "felt it and knew it was a boy." The same thing happened the second time around. Therefore, I was pretty certain the girl chance would be good.

When my brother Brian and I were kids I really wanted a sister and I nicknamed him Brianna. Brian is three and a half years younger than I am, and I used to dress him up in my clothes and put makeup on him. Somewhere I have an old photo that will make really good blackmail!

Something felt missing by not having a girl in my life. But that wasn't enough to talk me into having three kids. I was still worried about all of the practical aspects.

Can I have a career and three kids under school age? How will we pay for three kids in day care, sports, and college? Will we have enough room in our house? We'll have to get a minivan!

While I tend to worry about the details, Eirik is great about seeing the big picture. "Don't you want a large family? We both have small families and hardly any relatives. It would be so nice to have a big family as we grow older," he said. That was definitely not the perspective I had originally taken on the subject matter, but it made complete sense.

That October, I went with my mom to visit my brother and his wife and their two kids, Sam and Allie in California. They were pregnant with their third child. Since they live so far away, I hadn't gotten to know my niece and nephew very well. At the time, my niece was not quite two years old.

During that visit I put her hair in cute pigtails. I helped her get dressed in pink girly-girl outfits. I went with her to gymnastics class.

My brother looked at me and said, "You want one, don't you?"

"What do you mean?" I replied.

"You want a girl. You *need* a girl," he said.

"Yeah, I do," I blushed.

When I returned from that trip, I looked at Eirik and said, "Okay, let's go for it!" Of course I knew full well that the baby could be a boy, but I decided that while I might be disappointed, I would love any child and that a large family seemed right for us. So on Halloween night of 2008, we made the scary decision to become parents once again.

One cold blustery day in January, just after the excitement of the holidays had ended, I decided to take a day off and stay home from work. Eirik was working and the boys were at day care. I didn't quite know what to do with myself in the rare situation I was faced with: all alone in a quiet house.

I paced around the house wanting to take another pregnancy test, but I knew that Eirik would be disappointed if he wasn't there.

I had taken two pregnancy tests earlier in the week and they were both negative, but I couldn't help feeling like they were wrong. In fact, with both previous pregnancies the first few tests were a false negative.

The suspense was killing me! I am one of those people that need to open things up immediately because the anticipation of an unopened package makes me go crazy.

When Eirik and I got married several gifts were mailed to us before the wedding. Unfortunately for Eirik, all the gifts were opened and put away before he ever got a chance to see them.

I couldn't control the suspense any longer.

The test will probably be negative anyway, and then Eirik will never need to know I took the test without him.

I gave into my burning desire to want an answer immediately and took another pregnancy test. This time it was positive!

Then I got really sad because I was all alone and didn't have anyone to share the good news with. I didn't want to call Eirik and tell him at work or over e-mail, but I was dying to tell someone.

I decided to go shopping instead and find a cute way to surprise the family. I bought a pink shopping bag and put the pregnancy test inside, along with a pacifier, candy, and some other baby items. I decided to make spaghetti dinner that night. That would have been enough of a surprise to my husband since cooking is not my favorite thing to do.

When we all sat down at the dinner table, I handed him the pink bag. He really had no clue at first. It's funny how I can surprise him with things, like the time I pulled off a huge surprise party for his fortieth birthday. We had this romantic dinner while the entire time our guests were walking in right behind us, but he never suspected a thing. He can never surprise me with anything because I'm always questioning things and want answers.

"Really, is it true?" he exclaimed.

He was excited but a little disappointed.

"You didn't wait for me," he said as I suspected he would.

With the first two pregnancies, I took the test when he was home so we could watch the stick change color together.

"Well, this time it's going to be different," I proclaimed.

Boy, was that an understatement!

The early weeks of the pregnancy went about how I expected them to. I was so tired that as soon as the boys were in bed at seven thirty, I passed out on the couch and stayed there for about twelve hours. And just like my other pregnancies, the smell of coffee repulsed me. So much for staying awake from caffeine! I normally love coffee and my favorite guilty pleasure is a Caribou Coffee Skinny Vanilla Latte.

Right before our twenty-week ultrasound I worked at a neighborhood garage sale. They had tons of cute baby girl things for sale. I decided to take my chances and buy a tiny dress with hot pink flowers and a light pink hand-knit blanket. After all, if I was wrong, I could always sell them back at next year's garage sale, I reasoned with myself.

When we went in for our ultrasound, we couldn't wait to find out if we were right about the baby being a girl. With both of our other children we had a boy and a girl name picked out for the twenty-week ultrasound and then happily announced the name to our family at that time.

This time we were really stuck between two girls' names—Audrey Sophia or Emily Sophia. The name Sophia we wanted for sure. It is Jewish tradition to name a baby after a deceased relative. While my Aunt Sophie was still alive, she was ninety-four years old and we really wanted to name the baby after her, so we broke tradition.

The ultrasound technician put the freezing cold jelly on my belly and took a look around.

"When are we going to find out the gender?" I asked eagerly.

The technician said we needed to wait because the baby wouldn't cooperate. I was practically crawling out of my skin with nervous anticipation.

"No, we're not leaving here until we find out!" I practically shouted at the woman.

I was not about to wait twenty more weeks to find out if I could start shopping for dresses or painting the room pink.

A few minutes later she said, "I found it. It's a girl!"

I let out the biggest gasp imaginable and said, "Are you absolutely sure?"

After all, I didn't want to go pink crazy only to be disappointed later on.

"Oh yeah, it's definitely a girl," she said.

At that moment I let out a huge sigh, and then tears started streaming down my face. I don't think I even shed a tear during the birth of my two sons. The ultrasound technician printed us a souvenir picture of the girl parts and labeled it girl. I was elated to be having a baby girl!

But just as I was trying to catch my breath and let the good news sink in, the technician asked me to get up and go to the bathroom. When I came back from the bathroom, my obstetrician friend Regina was there.

"Regina, we're having a girl!" I exclaimed.

I thought she was there to hear the good news, but she had a serious look on her face.

"I'm so happy for you guys. Congratulations!" Regina said. "She looks great, and her growth is just perfect for twenty weeks. But, there is one thing that I would like to take a closer look at," she continued. "We are seeing three cysts in a part of the brain called the choroid plexus. This is the only abnormal finding we see, so I have a feeling that it isn't anything to worry about. If we were to see these cysts in conjunction with other abnormal findings, we might start to worry about something like Down syndrome; thankfully, we are not seeing any of the other findings. Because of your age, I'd like to send you to the perinatal clinic to have a comprehensive ultrasound to take another look," she said.

Suddenly, our joy turned to fear. I felt so selfish for only being concerned about the gender and not even considering the possibility that there could be something more serious identified on the ultrasound. I had taken it for granted that our first two children were born healthy.

Going to the perinatal clinic was a terrifying experience. Before we had the ultrasound, we were brought into a little office for a meeting.

"Do you know why you're here today?" the genetics counselor said.

"Because there is a cyst on her brain and it could be a sign of Down syndrome," I replied.

"Actually, we're looking for more than just Down syndrome," she said. "We're looking for any trisomy, some of which can be even more devastating than Down syndrome," she said. The counselor went on, "Some trisomies are even life threatening."

She then explained that a trisomy is a genetic abnormality in which there are three copies, instead of the normal two, of a particular chromosome.

Okay, now I was terrified out of my wits! During this two-hour meeting we were asked what our plans would be if we were given bad news. We were beyond the gestation for legalized abortion, but we really didn't have any intention of terminating the pregnancy and really wished we didn't even have to think about it.

When we went into the ultrasound, there was a large plasma screen television where we could view the baby right in front of us. Within minutes we were told that the cysts had resolved and that the remainder of the anatomy looked perfectly healthy. What a relief! The good news out of all of this is we got a CD of the 3D ultrasound as a keepsake. I'm sure glad it was something we'll want to see again!

The rest of the pregnancy was smooth sailing. I craved Chipotle fajita burritos all of the time. One day I went to eat one and got really sick. I left my purse at the table and ran to the bathroom and puked. After that, I was done with Chipotle and haven't eaten there since.

At first we decided on the name Audrey. We even received a beautiful gift before she was born—an embroidered bib and diaper cover with the name Audrey on it.

Then we started wavering a bit on the name. We kept surveying everyone we knew, "What do you think, Audrey or Emily?"

Eithan voted for Audrey and Evan voted for Emily.

After a few months of discussion, we decided to officially call her Emily Sophia. It was really cute because Eithan couldn't say Emily at the time and would say Elamee. We even considered that name and different variations or spellings of Emily such as Emilee, but we ended up settling on the traditional spelling.

During the seventh month I decorated the nursery two colors—pink and pinker! Two walls were painted hot pink and the other two a Pepto-Bismol pink. I decorated the walls with stick on flowers in lavender, hot pink, and yellow. I put the letters E-M-I-L-Y in white wood above the crib. The room was coordinated with a set of window shams, a blanket, a crib bumper, and a dust ruffle—all in bright pink, lavender, and yellow with matching flowers. I found the perfect hot pink rug to put on the oak wood floor. I also found white window sheers to soften the look. On the wall also hung wooden cursive letters that read *Princess* and *Love*. This was definitely a room made for a girl and it was just perfect, as I knew she would be.

One night, when I was thirty-six weeks pregnant, I woke up around three in the morning with an intense pain in my right side. It hurt so badly I thought the baby was stabbing my insides with a knife. The pain lasted about fifteen minutes until I turned over to my left side, and then it immediately went away.

The next morning, I was on my way to work when I decided to call the doctor's office and let them know what happened. The nurse said to come in right away. I turned my car around and got to the clinic as fast as I could.

When I arrived, the nurse hooked me up to a machine that monitors the baby and I learned that the pain was from the position of the baby irritating a nerve.

She also discovered that I was contracting every few minutes. I hadn't noticed the contractions until I sat quietly alone in the doctor's office.

Between working and running around with a two- and four-year-old, I don't think I was ever in a quiet enough place to pay any attention to my body.

"Are you ready to have your baby today?" said the nurse.

"What?" I exclaimed.

My boys were both a week late so this was totally unexpected.

I had already planned the birth date. I'm not someone who likes to waiver from plans once I make them, so this was particularly stressful. I was hoping Regina would deliver the baby on September 25, one week before the due date via elective induction. That way we could have the baby on a Friday and the family could visit on the weekend. Plus, it would fall two days after my mom's sixtieth birthday and right in between the Jewish holidays Rosh Hashanah and Yom Kippur. It was planned, perfectly planned, and that's the way I wanted it to be.

Eirik and I had debated the elective induction idea for months, and I had won the battle. I wanted to do it because I was worried about a quick labor and having to find last-minute care for the boys. It was also helpful to plan my last day at work to wrap things up nicely before my maternity leave. Finally, with both boys being a week overdue, the prospect of having the baby a week early seemed delightful.

Eirik was initially against the idea saying, "It's not right for us to decide the baby's birthday."

He caved, however, because he knew it was my body going through it and I felt so strongly about having a planned induction. I think the real truth was that he didn't want to deal with my bitchiness again during the forty-first week!

I called my husband at work from the doctor's office and told him the baby might be coming early. We were both going to be leaving work early that day to take Eithan to a hospital on the other side of town for a medical test.

"Oh my God, which hospital do I go to?" Eirik exclaimed.

"I don't know yet," I explained. "I'll call you back after I talk to the doctor. He wants to examine me to see if I'm dilated yet. Just start driving and I'll call you back and tell you which hospital to go to."

When the doctor examined me I found out I wasn't dilated at all.

"Nope, this isn't the real deal," he said.

I had never had Braxton-Hicks contractions with my first two children so this was a totally bizarre experience.

He ended up going east and heading to Eithan's appointment. I figured at least I was at a hospital if anything should change. During Eithan's visit I kept noticing the contractions, which made me really nervous and edgy. At least if they were happening before I wasn't aware of them so they weren't bothering me at all.

A few weeks later I couldn't sleep at all that night. It was a cool September evening yet I was sweating like crazy, and I rarely break a sweat, not even at the gym; so I knew that something was happening to my body.

Then I started feeling the contractions coming. It was Saturday morning and the boys were just waking up. Within a few minutes the contractions were just minutes apart.

I called the on-call doctor, who happened to be Regina's older sister, and she said to come into the hospital right away. We gathered up the whole family and went to labor and delivery.

Things certainly weren't going as planned! I had planned all three pregnancies. I really wanted the birth of this child to be planned too. I called Regina on her cell phone. She was home alone with her kids but she would try to get to the hospital as soon as possible.

When I arrived, the nurse checked me, and I was only one centimeter dilated.

One fucking centimeter, are you kidding me?

It was three weeks before my official due date, and if I made any cervical change, we were going to have a baby that day.

The nurses hooked me up to the fetal monitor and we waited and waited. The contractions continued to come every one to two minutes, but I remained at one centimeter. With Evan I was dilated to two centimeters for the last month of my pregnancy, so I wasn't feeling very confident about the progress at this point.

I asked the nurse to induce me. I just wanted to get this the hell over with! I knew from experience that babies are much easier on the inside than the outside, but I was growing impatient with the frequent and mildly painful contractions. It was like dinner was over and I just wanted to move on to dessert, even though you usually feel better about dessert before you eat it. The nurse said she couldn't induce me since it was too soon before my due date.

Meanwhile, the boys were in the room waiting for my mom to come pick them up and they were pretty scared watching Mommy in the hospital. I felt helpless lying in the hospital bed not being able to play with them.

They were getting really antsy and started tearing around like a couple of monkeys who just got let out of the cage. The nurse asked us if someone could *please* come pick them up. After what seemed like an eternity, Nana arrived.

After six hours, I was sent home with some sleeping pills. I was told that if it was real labor, I wouldn't sleep through it. I went home and passed out for twelve hours. Oh well, better luck next time. At least I finally got a good night's sleep!

A few days later I went to girls' night at my friend Dawn's house. Four of us from high school get together each month to catch up on life. It is great how we're all such good friends almost twenty years after graduation. We have gone through so much together—college, dating, marriage, divorce, kids, buying our first house, and turning into grownups (we're almost there).

As I was driving home that evening, I felt more contractions coming on. They got worse the closer I got to home during the half-hour drive. I figured they were just Braxton-Hicks contractions again and I tried to ignore them. I played a little Barenaked Ladies and tried to let the music drown out my fear.

When I got home, Eirik and I decided to relax and watch *Arrested Development* on TV. We just finished our show and were getting ready for bed when I felt the contractions starting again. This was a weird déjà vu since this was the exact way both of my boys were born.

When I went into labor the other two times, Eirik and I watched TV. With Evan we watched a repeat of *Friends* on DVD and with Eithan we saw *Dharma and Greg*. I went in to labor both times at ten pm, just as we were getting ready for bed. The contractions came, and they came on strong! Evan was born five hours later and Eithan four hours later.

Since it happened again at 10:00 pm, right after we watched TV and as we were getting ready for bed, we decided this must be the way it was meant to happen. I decided I could live with the change of plans.

Just get this damn baby out!

I called my dad's cousin Shelly, who is retired and lives about ten minutes away, to warn her that we may need her to come over and stay with the boys.

I called Regina and she told me to go to the hospital immediately, that she suspected this time it would be for real. We waited outside on the driveway for Shelly to arrive on this warm September evening, just as she had for Eithan's birth. We then drove like hell on the all-too familiar route to the hospital.

When we got there I was dilated to two centimeters, so it was looking more hopeful this time. We were sent to the same labor and delivery room where Eithan was born, so I figured that must be a sign.

Even though I told them to wait until we had confirmation that this was the real deal, my parents and great-aunt Sophie drove the forty-five minutes to the hospital to witness the birth of their fifth and final grandchild. I nicknamed her *The Grand Finale*.

The nurse hooked me up to a fetal monitor and I prepared to give birth one last time. Once again I had continuous contractions, every one to two minutes, but I remained at two centimeters.

Two centimeters, bloody hell!

They wanted to send me home but I was determined to have this baby. I wanted the annoying contractions to stop and I didn't want to leave the hospital putting in all of the work with nothing to show for it! I am very results-oriented and like to have visual confirmation of my efforts.

They told me to walk around the hospital. My anxious family members kept asking me what was going on and in a tone that's very unlike me I snapped at them, "Leave me the hell alone!"

As I walked around the hospital in my gown and slippers, I cursed at all of the women I heard giving birth. "I got here first," I whined like a four-year-old!

When my parents told me they had met some nice folks whose daughter had just given birth, I snarled at them and said it wasn't fair and that I wasn't happy for them at all.

The nurse wanted to send me home, but I told her I wanted to wait a little longer because I felt like this was the real thing. I would not give up this time, I just wouldn't!

I lay on my right side and took a nap while Eirik sat and held my hand. I squeezed him tightly every time I felt a contraction. He was so calm and supportive while I was anxious and bitchy. We waited until about three in the morning and finally accepted defeat.

Maybe things were going to go as planned after all.

The boys are getting excited for the arrival of their baby sister. Who could have predicted our world would get so shaken up in just a few short weeks?

CHAPTER 4

The Birth

Sometimes things really do go as planned. For me, things went my way on September 25, 2009.

That morning, Regina was going to induce me into labor. It was a cool and rainy day. I was happy about that because if I was going to be in the hospital for a few days, I didn't want to miss any good weather.

I got up at 6:00 am and called the hospital to make sure there was a room available. The nurse said that they were short staffed that morning and to call back in a few hours.

Oh no, not again! I thought to myself. *I just want to get this bun out of the oven!*

We were told ahead of time that elective inductions were based on staff availability and could be delayed if the labor unit was full, so I knew that our preferred date wasn't guaranteed.

Since there wasn't much I could do except anxiously wait around, I decided to go back to sleep realizing this would be the last few hours I could willingly sleep for a while.

Around 7:30 am, the nurse called my cell phone and told me to come in right away. I was not ready at all and the boys were surprisingly still sound asleep. I scrambled to get dressed and wake them up. We still had to drive them to day care, but luckily it was en route to the hospital.

We made it to the hospital by 8:30 in the morning where Regina had been waiting for us for a while. We felt like VIPs having our doctor come right away to greet us rather than at pushing time.

Once we got settled in, Regina returned to the clinic which was attached to the hospital. The nurse offered me lavender-scented towels for relaxation. This thrilled me to no end as lavender is my absolute favorite scent.

I'll pretend I'm at the spa. Now about that massage, Eirik?

The nurse immediately started an IV, which was extremely painful for some strange reason. After a little while I could barely move my arm it hurt so badly. In fact, the pain in my hand bothered me more than the labor pains. Maybe that was a good thing because it distracted me from what was happening down below.

Around 11:00 am, things were moving slowly. By this time my parents and my great-aunt Sophie had arrived at the hospital. I told them to go have lunch because it was going to be awhile.

Eirik and my dad went to Taco Bell, which was right outside of the hospital, while my mom took Aunt Sophie to Target. She had recently given up driving and needed a few essentials.

As soon as they left, the contractions came on painfully hard. I called for the nurse and she came in the room.

"My husband just left, please hold my hand!" I yelled.

She squeezed my hand tightly and told me it would be okay. I squeezed her hand back so hard she probably couldn't feel it for a week. I'm sure I left her a few bruises.

At this time I asked for an epidural. I tried to call my husband on his cell phone to tell him to come back to the hospital, but he didn't answer.

"Of all times for him not to answer his fucking phone!" I yelled.

Man, was I pissed! Then I called my dad who picked up.

"Come back right now!" I yelled into the receiver.

My husband reentered the room just as they were putting the needle into my spine.

"I'm so sorry," he said, "But you told me to leave. I feel so bad, what did I miss?"

"Apparently that was a dumb idea," I responded, pointing at the gigantic needle they were inserting into me.

Shortly after the epidural, Regina stopped back in and said, "I think you have a few hours still. I'll come back later."

Nothing happened for a while, so I just rested. I couldn't believe I was able to relax, but by the third time in the hospital I was out of energy. Then all of the sudden, I awoke from my nap and felt the baby crowning.

Get the doctor *now!*" I shouted.

Regina ran down the hall as fast as she could just in time to catch the baby's head as it was making an appearance. All I could see were black patent leather clogs.

"She looks just like Eithan," Regina said as the baby entered this crazy mixed-up world of ours.

We officially declared her name Emily Sophia. She was born at exactly 2:00 pm and weighed six pounds eleven ounces. She was the perfect little bundle of joy with olive-colored skin, bright blue eyes, and fuzzy light brown hair. I just looked at her in amazement.

For the first time, I was able to hold my baby immediately after birth. Both of my boys had meconium in their amniotic fluid, and the nurses needed to examine them before I could hold them.

She was instantly hungry and latched onto me immediately. We seemed to bond right away.

The next day was filled with friends and family coming to visit. It was a very joyous time and everything seemed to be going smoothly, or so I thought.

When I spoke about this day to Aunt Sophie, she said that I seemed very quiet and distant. I remember feeling a little annoyed at the visitors' chattiness, but I would have been more upset if no one had come to visit.

Back at home, things were anything but joyous. Eithan was in the midst of a major asthma episode. When he gets these attacks it usually takes several weeks for him to fully recover.

I started worrying that Eithan was going to be hospitalized and that he would be on another floor and the family would have to visit both of us and poor Emily wouldn't get the attention she deserved. I wondered if the hospital would wheel me up to visit him. I felt horrible mom-guilt for not being there during this time. It was killing me. I am the one who always handles his medical issues, and I didn't have any control over the situation.

My mom was staying with the boys at our house while we were in the hospital with baby Emily. I prayed that she would know how to handle whatever situation arose.

What if she forgets to give him his meds and he quits breathing? I left three pages of notes, but what if she doesn't understand my directions?

I started thinking about the mess that I had left the house in, and how without me there it would be even worse. I'd have to come home with a newborn and two little boys and clean. I worried that my children wouldn't eat properly, or get played with enough.

Are they getting the attention they deserve?

I thought about the dishes I left in the sink.

They must be rotting by now.

I didn't like this feeling of not being able to control what was going on at home.

Later that night, Eirik started to feel ill. He came down with a fever and could barely stand. It was right at the height of the H1N1 epidemic and the hospital was being overprotective and not letting children or anyone with a cold visit.

People all over our city were getting sick and earlier that week several schools had closed for fear of the disease spreading. The H1N1 vaccine still wasn't available and everyone was paranoid about the disease, which was one of the worst strains of the flu ever to hit our country.

I told Eirik to go home and get some sleep and that we would be fine. He left and went back to the boys while my mom came to see me and Emily.

While I told him to go home and that everything would be fine, I lied. I felt empty and abandoned by my husband. I desperately wanted him there to share in this experience.

Why the hell did he have to get sick and leave me? Is this a sign of things to come? Is he going to leave me alone to raise three children? I can't do that; I can't even take care of myself most of the time.

After he left, I was exhausted and went to sleep early. I awoke in the middle of the night in a panic. My heart raced and I trembled in fear. I thought someone had punched me in the chest. I shot straight out of the hospital bed and checked my Blackberry to see if there were any messages from Eirik. I e-mailed him several times in the middle of the night asking how he was, but he never replied.

Oh my God, my husband has H1N1! He's going to be in the hospital, Eithan is going to be in the hospital and I'm going to be left all alone to take care of everyone! What if Eirik were to die? I would be a thirty-five-year-old widow left with three kids. We wouldn't have any money and we would have to live in a shelter. The kids would wear tattered clothes and be teased at school.

While I didn't realize what was happening at the time, this was my first real panic attack. At the time I didn't even know what a panic attack was, but a few months later my psychiatrist explained that people experiencing panic attacks often have symptoms, such as labored breathing, heart palpitations, nausea, chest pain, feelings of choking and smothering, dizziness, sweating, and trembling. Some people may even experience depersonalization (a feeling of being outside one's body), derealization (a feeling of the world's not real), and fears of losing control, of going crazy, or even of dying.

Meanwhile, Eirik went to urgent care to get himself checked out. I tried texting and calling him about fifty times that morning, but he was busy being thoroughly evaluated at the doctor's office and wasn't answering my messages. I wanted answers! I was stuck in the hospital bed and I couldn't control what was happening to my husband or my kids.

Please God, help me!

It turns out he didn't have H1N1, but he did have strep throat. He was not allowed back in the hospital for fear of exposing other patients. Plus, he felt miserable.

I called him and told him not to come home, that he must stay at his sister's house or at a hotel. He would expose the baby and Eithan in his vulnerable state, and then everyone would be doomed.

I called his sister in a panic, along with Regina, my mom and dad, and Eirik's mom. I told them I couldn't go home. I felt that going home would be an impossible situation, one that I tremendously feared.

Eirik was not at all pleased by my idea of staying at his sister's house and protested my pleas. He wanted to be home with his family, not held prisoner in someone else's home.

When the pediatrician came to take a final look at Emily before our discharge, I burst into tears again telling him that I couldn't go home; that I couldn't handle a sick husband, a sick two-year-old, and a newborn. He told me that he also has kids and it can be stressful, but that a newborn can't catch strep throat and that there's nothing to worry about.

I was terrified by the situation. I wondered what the hell I had gotten myself into and really didn't want to bring this baby home. I wished I could send her back.

What's the return policy? Do I get ninety days to see if I like her?

I called my mom and asked if she could stay for a few days and she agreed to do so.

I was reaching out to everyone, yet there was no rope to grab. No one understood what was really going on inside my head. How could they, I didn't even understand what was happening.

I continued sobbing and imagining my baby contracting an awful disease and me not being able to do anything about it. It would be better if she was never born than to die so young. As someone who likes to control things, this situation felt completely out of my control.

I paged the hospital nurse to come to my room. When she arrived, I pleaded with her that I needed to stay another night; that there was no way I could go home and take care of everyone.

The nurse said that there was nothing medically wrong with me. I had experienced an uncomplicated vaginal birth and I needed to be released that morning, according to hospital policy.

My sister-in-law Penny called to see if she could visit the baby and I told her we were being discharged and I needed a ride home. When she arrived, I lost it again.

This wasn't the happy homecoming it was supposed to be. We were supposed to go home as husband and wife and have a joyous time introducing our new baby to her big brothers. The *plan* went wrong, which doesn't sit well for planners like me.

At home, Eirik was sequestered in the basement with a surgical mask. We finally agreed that he could come home as long as he didn't go near the kids. When I arrived with the baby, he came upstairs and stood on the other side of the room taking pictures as Emily and her brothers met for the first time.

When I look at the photos and the video he took now, you can tell that they were taken from a long distance. Our joy of having a baby was squashed by all of the other stresses going on in our lives at that time.

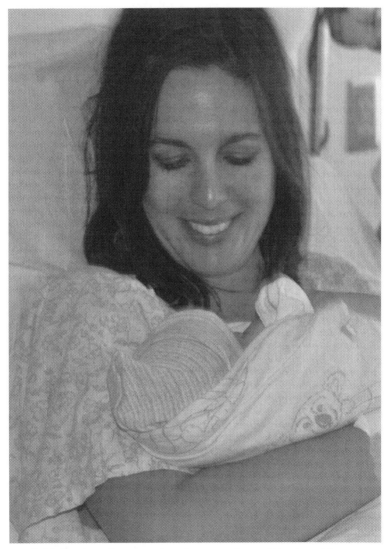

I felt happy when my daughter was born. I had no idea at this time the rocky road that we were in for.

CHAPTER 5

The First Few Weeks

Since Emily was an easygoing baby, I expected our transition home to be like a graceful ballet dance, not a roller-coaster ride with unexpected twists and turns followed by a major decline. After all, we knew what we were doing by baby number three (or so we thought).

When we brought the baby home we put her in a Pack 'n Play in our bedroom so I could easily nurse her and get back to sleep.

Sleep, what a joke! Every time the baby so much as breathed, I would pick her up and feed her. I was *paranoid* that she'd disturb her brothers and that the whole house would be awake. Then I would have to deal with two crabby toddlers as well as a new baby, which was way more than I could handle!

Just about every hour on the hour I nursed her and didn't get any sleep in between because I kept anticipating the next feeding.

I was determined, despite the lack of sleep, to carry on a normal routine for the boys. When Emily was just a few days old, I brought Evan and Eithan to Pump It Up, a play area with about a dozen jumpers for little kids. We stayed for at least a couple of hours, about as long as I could go without needing to get back to nurse my newborn.

No one even knew I had just had a baby. I hadn't gained a ton of weight with the pregnancy, and with the cool weather I was able to hide my flabby belly under big clothes.

Later that week, Evan had a school field trip to a local apple orchard. A parent was supposed to come, but siblings were not allowed. He was going to get to practice riding the big yellow school bus, something he would do every day next year during kindergarten. There was no way I was going to miss that special day. I mustered up as much energy as I could and went along, even though physically my body was dragging.

On the outside I appeared as together and intact as ever. His teachers were shocked that I had come.

"You look great," Miss Naomi said. "You don't even look like you just had a baby."

The other moms didn't even know that I had just given birth. When we were on the hayride I started talking to the other moms about my kids and mentioned that I had a brand new baby. They seemed shocked that I was so casually going about life as normal. I was really proud of myself for this accomplishment. A new baby wasn't going to get in my way!

During the field trip, I worried about Eirik taking care of the new baby and Eithan, who was still quite ill, and hoped that Emily wouldn't get hungry. I could feel my breasts swelling up. While I enjoyed the actual act of breast-feeding, I hated the dependency it caused. I really wanted my own body back and to be free.

I remember that day feeling like the people and everything around me seemed a little fuzzy and surreal, but I just blew it off to being tired. As I've learned more about my condition, it really was the first time I experienced disassociation, which is the state of being disconnected.

The following Monday, I took Eithan and the baby to his early childhood class. The other mothers looked at me in disbelief wondering why I would be running around like that after just giving birth.

I recall one mom saying, "I could never do that. When I had my baby, I stayed at home for months."

I thought she was absolutely crazy. Why would anyone stay home just because they had a new baby? I felt like that would be really unfair to my older children, and having done this twice before, I thought I could handle my normal routine, though some people say they could never keep up with my schedule on any given day.

A week after Emily's birth, the hospital sent out a home health nurse to evaluate my condition and the baby's. This service was covered by my insurance and I decided to take the hospital up on their offer. I had never had this type of visit with my previous births.

The nurse, Betty, was an older woman, a grandma type. I recall her having a big silver cross around her neck and long hair. Betty reminded me of a nun. Her children were grown and she visited new moms on a daily basis all across town.

Evan was at preschool during this visit and Eithan was playing nicely on the floor in front of me as I held baby Emily and we talked at the kitchen table. Everything in our household looked calm and peaceful on the outside.

She told me that the first two weeks after giving childbirth is a recovery period for a woman and that a lot of rest and help are essential for your health.

While I believed what she was saying, it seemed impossible to stay home and rest for two weeks. After all, I had two older children and numerous commitments.

One of the assessments Nurse Betty gave me was a set of standardized questions to determine if I had postpartum depression.

Some of the questions from the screening were (Allina Hospitals & Clinics, Postpartum Depression Worksheet, 2006):

- Do you feel depressed or sad?
- Do you feel you can't do anything right?
- Do you have no real desire to eat or get enjoyment out of eating food?

I answered all of the questions with a firm no. I figured that postpartum depression was only for mentally unstable people to begin with and I felt I had my shit together. I passed with flying colors!

When Eirik got home from work that night, I told him what the nurse said about resting for two weeks.

"Promise me you'll help me do that," I said.

I knew I wouldn't rest or relax on my own. I don't think I even know how to do that. I really wanted him to encourage me to do so, because deep down I knew it was a good idea.

"Are you kidding!" he said. "There is no way I can ever get you to do that."

Eirik knows that I am a strong-willed independent woman and even if he told me to stay home and rest, I wouldn't listen. After all, I had to keep up my *Supermom* status.

Later that week, a nurse from the OB/GYN clinic called me for a postpartum depression check as they do with all new moms, which included a very similar screening as the home health nurse had conducted. I was surprised that I was getting all of these screenings—this was a big change in just a few years since my sons were born.

"You definitely don't have postpartum depression," she said.

I scored really well on the screening. I told them how well everything was going and how I was carrying on with life as normal. I also mentioned how impressed people were that I was so put together. I felt happy at my accomplishment of being a mom of three kids and not letting anything slow me down. I felt like this third child was a breeze and I was a little bit irritated that I had to do the postpartum depression screenings when I was obviously just fine.

When Emily was just a week and a half old, I received a call from an agent about a modeling job for Emily and me. My mom's cousin owns a modeling school and I had done a lot of work for her when I was a kid. Her grown daughters now run the agency and knew about Emily's birth.

"Do you know how old she is?" I told the agent, one of the employees at the agency.

"Yes, we are looking for newborns and their moms," she replied.

So at thirteen days old, I drove Emily across town early in the morning for a photo shoot. I was so tired and loved how my part involved lying down with my eyes closed and holding the baby on my chest.

When I look at these pictures I appear so at peace and relaxed on the outside, but in the inside I was a total train wreck. The photo shoot was a huge success and we ended up in a national Target Portrait Studios campaign.

To this day I can see Emily's picture when I go to Target and have found them appearing in several advertising campaigns. It's funny how deceiving those pictures really are—we look like the mother and daughter poster team for just given birth bliss.

I was supposed to go back to work after six weeks and at two weeks postpartum, the thought of it made me sick to my stomach.

How can I leave my little baby? How will I even function at work on no sleep?

I was working as a marketing consultant at the time, something I'm usually very passionate about; but after my daughter's birth I had absolutely no interest in helping small business owners with their marketing. It seemed so insignificant compared to raising my children.

I was in the process of trying to find a nanny to come into our home while I went to work, but I was really dreading the thought of a stranger taking care of my newborn baby.

I knew Emily would be our last child, and I really had a strong desire to be there with her for the first year. I always felt guilty about missing those early months with Eithan, having gone back to work when he was just eight weeks old.

I had meant to talk to Eirik about this feeling during the pregnancy, but we never seemed to find the time. We finally did sit down and talk one day when he was on paternity leave and we agreed that I would quit my job and try to find some part-time work from home for the next year.

I was relieved that I didn't have to go back to work, but worried about what I would do next and if we could handle it financially.

I was really nervous calling my boss, Greg, the owner of the firm. The entire company was only about thirty employees, so one person quitting was a big deal. I am usually true to my word and I felt guilty about changing my mind.

Greg was a great boss. During my interview with him he held a coffee mug that read *World's Greatest Dad*, so I knew he was a family guy. When I called Greg he completely understood my decision.

In talking with many of my friends with young children, it seems like I am not alone in this push-pull feeling we women have about choosing a career or a family. As progressive as our world seems as women, we still feel the responsibility to be the primary caregiver for our young children. We tend to feel guilty when we're at work and not with our kids, and we feel guilty when we're not contributing to the family's income or using our education and knowledge to its fullest potential.

When Emily was three weeks old, my brother Brian and his wife Erin and kids—Allie, then two and a half and Jack, then six months—came to visit from California. I was so excited for them to come since it had been two years since their last visit.

My brother and his family arrived at our house at 6:00 am. Of course, I was awake. I had cleaned the house and everything was perfect for their arrival.

We spent the day at our house chatting and catching up and I tried to hide the fact that I was exhausted beyond belief. I wanted to appear as if having a third child wasn't a big deal and we were just one big happy family. My anticipation of his arrival and wanting to appear put-together only deepened my anxiety.

At dinner time we drove to their hotel and met my parents. We decided to have pizza at the hotel's restaurant and take the kids swimming.

The restaurant had the slowest service I had ever experienced. It had been about an hour and a half and we still didn't have our pizza. I was growing increasingly agitated.

Before our food even arrived I took the baby back to my brother's hotel room to nurse her. She spit up on my clothes, her clothes, and on the hotel bed. I put on my mom's sweater but hated it because it was scratchy and made me itch.

When I came back to the restaurant, everyone had eaten and the pizza was cold. I started screaming and throwing a fit about how horrible the place was and that the waiter wasn't getting any tip from me.

This behavior was really out of character. I am normally very non-confrontational and don't like to cause any sort of conflict.

When we took the kids swimming I didn't have my swimsuit on, so I watched over them like a hawk from the edge of the pool. I was convinced they were going to die in that pool.

I had taken them swimming several times before and had never worried about their safety, but for some reason this night was different. I felt very out of control, especially because I wasn't in the water with them.

My husband and brother were both swimming and were perfectly capable of watching the children, but I didn't trust them. I wanted to jump in fully clothed and save them. I kept yelling at my husband and brother to watch them more carefully. I was terrified for their lives.

Eirik decided to take Evan to the larger pool and they were even further out of my line of vision, which caused even more anxiety.

Then I heard screaming and felt like my insides were going to explode. Evan was fine; he was just a little scared going down the water slide. In the process of trying to alleviate his fear, Eirik jumped into the pool with him and injured his knee while doing so.

Normally Eirik is the overprotective father and I am more laid-back when it comes to the kids' safety. That night, however, I was like a mother duckling trying to protect her eggs.

The next evening, my brother and his wife went to a wedding rehearsal dinner. I thought it would be fun if my niece slept over, and we also agreed to watch their baby for a few hours while they were gone. I really don't know how I thought taking care of five kids on no sleep would be fun.

I went to the store and got a Halloween cookie decorating kit for an activity that evening. The kids were so cute with orange and black frosting smeared all over their faces.

I took a bunch of pictures of Evan, Eithan, and Allie having some Halloween fun. They were so dirty that I decided to give them all a bath. Evan's face broke out in a terrible rash from the frosting. It looked like he had red frosting still stuck to his face even after I washed him.

We set up a slumber party in the basement for the three big kids. We had sleeping bags and pillows and turned on a movie so they could chill out for a while.

When it was time to go to sleep, Allie got terrified. She wanted her mommy and daddy back. Her parents ended up coming back in the middle of the night and taking her home.

Suddenly, I started feeling exhausted beyond belief. The three weeks of sleeplessness and running around like a mad woman were starting to take a toll on my body. I was not only tired but felt like I could barely function at all. I was also getting more and more irritated at everything and everyone around me.

CHAPTER 6

Getting Sick at Home

Sunday, October 18, 2009

I love parties. I *never* miss a chance to socialize. Something was very wrong the day I cancelled party plans.

It was Sunday morning and my mom had an open house to welcome my brother and his family to town. The entire extended family was going to be there. It was a day that everyone had looked forward to for a long time because no one had met baby Jack yet, and Allie was just a baby last time Brian and Erin visited. The family was also going to meet baby Emily for the first time, so it was a big celebration.

I woke up that morning with a terrible allergy attack. My eyes were watery and swollen and I couldn't stop sneezing. I took some allergy medicine and that seemed to help.

A few hours later, I was getting ready for the party and the room started spinning. I felt like I was drunk, stumbling across the living room, but I hadn't had anything to drink in months. When I walked, I felt dizzy. Things in the room started going in and out of focus and I started losing perspective. I decided to lie down on the couch for a while and that seemed to make things a lot better.

I can't miss the party; I have to get over this silly thing.

I called and had my obstetrician, Dr. Anderson, paged. He was the one who had seen me during my pregnancy. I told him what was going on. He couldn't find any medical reason as to why I should be dizzy. Then I remembered that I had taken the allergy medicine, which can have a sedating effect. Dr. Anderson thought the allergy medicine was probably having some side effect and said to just take it easy for a few hours—it was probably nothing.

I followed the doctor's orders and rested on the couch for a few more hours, leaving Eirik in charge of all three kids. Then I called my mom and told her there was no way I could make it to the party. I knew everyone was looking forward to meeting Emily, but I just wasn't up for it.

I walked up to bed and tried to take a nap. I had finally fallen asleep for a few hours when I heard this horrible crash. I got out of bed and looked down. There was Eirik lying at the bottom of the stairs moaning.

"What's going on?" I shouted.

"I threw out my back," he replied. "I'm trying to get up. I'm taking myself to urgent care."

I knew this was serious because like most men, he avoids doctors like the plague. He always tries to be a tough guy and says, "I'll be fine." He also hates to ask anyone for help and always tries to do everything himself.

"You can't drive yourself to urgent care!" I exclaimed. "You can't even move."

Then I realized I couldn't drive him either. I felt like I was drunk, and I would *never* drink and drive. It would be more of a risk for me to try and drive him to the clinic.

I decided to call my cousin Shelly who lives nearby to see if she'd left for the party yet. Our house was on the way. I asked if she could take us both to the doctor—that way they could check out Eirik's back and my dizziness at the same time. Instead, she ended up taking the boys to the party and her husband, Ron, took Eirik and me, along with baby Emily to the urgent care clinic.

When we got to the urgent care clinic it was busier than I'd ever seen it before. There were dozens of people wearing masks and coughing. Oh yeah, the height of H1N1. The virus ran through our community like a plague.

We waited and waited for what seemed like an eternity. I was paranoid that baby Emily would get sick. I covered her carrier with a blanket and tried to keep her at a distance from sick people, but there was really no place to go.

I anxiously paced around the urgent care waiting room, feeling like I was trapped in a terrible place and I couldn't keep my newborn safe. I started weighing the pros and cons of staying and decided that exposing Emily to H1N1 would only make our problems worse. I asked Ron to drive me and the baby home. Eirik decided to stay at the clinic and get checked out.

Ron came back to our house and watched some TV while I went up to bed with the baby. I couldn't sleep at all because I was concerned about Eirik. I was also not feeling quite like myself and it was bothering me that I couldn't figure out what was wrong.

I was really nervous about how we were going to take care of three kids when we couldn't even take care of ourselves. I felt very helpless, hopeless, and worried about everything. I was completely on edge and every little disruption that I normally handle with ease in life would set me off.

It had been a few more hours and we hadn't heard from Eirik.

Why the hell doesn't he answer his cell phone when I'm desperate to reach him?

I asked Ron to go back to the clinic to see what was happening. I finally got a hold of Eirik and he said he would walk home. He had pulled a muscle in his back while bending over to do laundry with our new front load washer and dryer. His knee had given out as he bent over (a result from the swimming accident) and twisted his back the wrong way.

"You're crazy to walk home!" I shouted.

The clinic was at least three miles away, and the last time I had seen him he couldn't even get off of the floor.

"It actually feels better when I walk," he said. "I just can't sit down at all or I'm in a lot of pain."

Ron found him on the street, about a mile from our house, and drove him the rest of the way home.

Monday, October 19, 2009

The next day was my brother's last day in town and I really wanted to make it a good one. I woke up feeling much better and we decided to take all five kids to the zoo.

Eirik took the day off of work because of his back pain and decided to join us. His back was okay as long as he kept moving. He just couldn't sit down!

I didn't drink coffee during my nine months of pregnancy, but that day I was hitting the coffee pot hard just to stay coherent. Caffeine was probably the worst thing I could have done for my body, since it triggers anxiety, but it was my one vice.

We spent several hours at the zoo and had a really great time. My mood was a lot steadier that day and the dizziness had subsided.

This photo was taken of Eirik and me during our trip to the zoo. He had just thrown out his back and I was experiencing dizzy spells. This was less than a week before my hospitalization.

Later that afternoon while rocking Emily to sleep, I called my neighbor Ashley to ask her how things were going with her new baby. Ashley gave birth to a baby girl two weeks before me.

Ashley started telling me how she took medication for postpartum depression. She said she had postpartum depression with her second child, and she wasn't taking any chances this time around. She decided not to nurse her baby at all so she could stay on her regular antidepressant, which isn't safe for breast-feeding.

It was at this moment that I realized things were not going as smoothly as I had originally thought during this postpartum period, and maybe I needed to learn more about postpartum depression.

"How do you know if you have postpartum depression?" I asked.

"I feel like crying all of the time. I just don't care about anything anymore," she answered.

"I wonder if I have postpartum depression," I asked her, but my symptoms were so different from Ashley's.

I really wanted to know what was wrong because I didn't feel like myself.

"I haven't been crying or anything, but something just feels off," I told her.

She suggested I talk to my doctor. Maybe they could recommend something.

I called the clinic and spoke to a nurse. She urged me to come in right away. I explained that I was really busy but would come in at the end of the week when my schedule freed up a bit.

The nurse must have recognized that I wasn't doing well, because she recommended that I go to the emergency room. I thought she was crazy. This wasn't an emergency; I was just a little dizzy. I thought the nurse had overreacted to the situation, and without seeing me she didn't really know what she was talking about.

I wondered what I sounded like on the phone that made her react this way. She must have realized that my dizziness didn't have any physical explanation, because she also told me to make an appointment with a counselor who specializes in postpartum depression to discuss the situation.

Once again, I thought this was overkill, but I made the phone call anyway. The counselor was no longer at the clinic, so I gave up. I could have gone on the Internet and looked for help, but I was too sick and too tired to dig any further.

Finally, she suggested that I take an antidepressant that was safe for breast-feeding, and explained to me that it would take up to four weeks to start working. Four weeks sounded like an eternity, so I decided not to fill the prescription.

A doctor that I had never met before called me back later that afternoon. She had gotten a report of my condition from my call to the nurse.

"You don't have any of the symptoms of depression, and it sounds like you are just stressed out and need more sleep. You don't need to be on medication at this point," she said.

I was relieved to hear that I didn't have postpartum depression and it was just fatigue that I was experiencing.

Tuesday, October 20, 2009

The next day the dizziness got worse. I started feeling like I was really drunk and it was colliding with being overcaffeinated. My body started fighting with itself.

I called the doctor's office again and they suggested I take the antianxiety medicine that the nurse had mentioned earlier. Once again, I decided to skip the medicine. I hate taking any kind of medicine because I don't like my body feeling altered and not in my control. Besides, it seemed pointless to take something that wouldn't work for a month when I was feeling rotten *now*. I wanted a solution that would immediately fix my problem because my level of functioning was rapidly worsening.

I still didn't really believe that I had a mental issue. I was convinced it was a physical ailment. The mental issue seemed so vague to me, and there was no real way to prove it existed.

Eirik came home from work that night and surprised me with a gift—a membership to the gym that he had joined earlier that year.

"This will help relieve some stress," he said. "They even have a child care center where you can leave the kids and have some time to yourself."

I was really excited by this gift and wanted to start yoga classes right away to relieve some of my stress. I desperately wanted to believe that a few hours at the gym could make everything go back to normal again.

That night Eithan's asthma got much worse. Besides being up feeding the baby, I was up all night giving him breathing treatments. I was so tired that I didn't know which end was up. I just went from Eithan's room back to Emily's Pack 'n Play, sometimes forgetting which child I had just tended to.

Wednesday, October 21, 2009

The next morning I had a job interview. Good God, how did I think I would ever pull off a job interview in this condition! I was trying my best to function as if everything was fine, but I was far from fine. I don't know if this was denial, or just not knowing what to do, but I felt the need to lead my life as usual. I thought if I did this, I'd feel like myself.

I went to the interview feeling jittery as hell. It was like I had had fifteen cups of Starbucks espresso! I know I talked a mile a minute and couldn't focus on what the interviewer was even saying. I was starting to feel less and less like myself.

What's happening to me?

After the interview, I picked up Evan from preschool and decided to take him to Wendy's for lunch and a little one-on-one time.

"Mommy, this is the best day ever!" he said.

Right then I realized how hard having a new baby in the house was on my other little ones and that mother guilt stabbed me in the heart. Evan was doing a great job acting as the big-big brother, but I'm sure the lack of attention between the newborn and his sick brother was affecting him greatly. I felt really bad that he was the one getting ignored through all of the chaos.

When I came home from lunch with Evan, I found two-year-old Eithan sitting at a chair trying to eat his lunch. He was slurring his words and talking baby talk. This was really strange because he had been able to speak in clear sentences for quite some time.

Then I saw his eyes roll back. I immediately called my dad, who had been babysitting, and asked him what was going on with Eithan. He said that he had been talking baby talk for a while, but he thought he was just trying to be cute.

I knew something serious was happening. I decided to get him to eat, hoping that a little food would change things. Then I brought him up to his bed and observed him for a little while. Something was definitely wrong. I thought about all of the medications that he was on.

Oh my God! What did I give him?

I was so tired and out of it that I wasn't sure if I'd even given him the right dosages. He was on so many medications and I was becoming increasingly confused.

I tried calling Christa, the nurse at his pulmonologist's office whom I always call for dosage information when he has an asthma attack. She was at lunch.

"Damn it!" I shouted.

I decided that I must have overdosed him and called poison control. They told me to call 911 and get a paramedic over immediately.

When the paramedics arrived, I was in hysterics.

"Please don't take away my kids! I didn't mean to do it!" I pleaded.

"We aren't going to take away your kids, lady," said the officer. "You just look like a very sleep-deprived new mom. Why don't you get some rest?" he said.

While the paramedics were there, Eithan had gone from slowed down to sped up. He was racing through the house like a crazy person. He grabbed a wooden step stool from the bathroom and lifted it over his head running full speed ahead through the house. I was terrified that he would hurt his baby sister in the process. I immediately put her upstairs in the Pack 'n Play and closed the door. She started crying hysterically.

I tried calling Eirik at work, but once again he didn't answer his phone. I went on a rampage and started texting Eirik about a million times saying, "Get the fuck home now!" This was totally out of character. A few months later, he showed me those messages on his phone and I was in disbelief—it didn't sound like me at all!

After the paramedics left, I called Regina and told her what was going on. I read her the paramedic's notes and she said that Eithan would be fine, but she was very concerned about me.

When Nurse Christa called me back, she said I had given Eithan his medications correctly.

"I think you just have a bad case of postpartum depression," she said.

I talked more about it to my dad and I found out that he had given Eithan a giant caramel apple. Eithan hadn't eaten breakfast that morning, and that on top of his medications might have affected his blood sugar.

I called Eithan's pediatrician to explain what had happened and she thought he had experienced a seizure. I was too sick at the time to take him to the doctor, so I just let it go. To this day, I still have no idea what really happened because my state of mind was so fuzzy at that time.

That afternoon we were supposed to do a modeling job for Eirik, myself, and Emily. It was something that we had been planning for a few weeks and were really excited about. I had bought us all new white and black shirts, jeans, socks, and accessories to wear to the photo shoot. It was one of the few things that seemed to be going well at that point in our lives, and I didn't want to blow it.

Being someone that *hates* changing plans, I actually tried to figure out how we could get there after the paramedics left. Then I looked in the mirror and saw my blotchy red face, swollen eyes, and messy hair and realized that this wasn't the day. Not to mention the fact that Eirik's back still hurt and Eithan was really sick. Eirik called the agency and let them know we had a family emergency.

Eirik left work in the middle of a meeting that afternoon to come home and see what was going on. When he walked in, I immediately went down to the basement and put myself in solitary confinement. I just couldn't stop feeling guilty about what had happened to Eithan earlier that day.

Even if I hadn't poisoned him, how could I let my son get that sick?

I felt like a terrible mother. I didn't think I was suitable to raise my kids and thought they'd be better off without me. My therapist calls this Escapist Fantasy, which is a common trait in postpartum mood disorders in which moms fantasize about leaving everything.

That night Eirik urged me to get out of the house and take some time for myself. I decided I would have dinner, see a movie, and relax in the hot tub at the gym—alone.

I went to Panera, one of my favorite places to eat. But instead of relaxing as I should have, I spent an hour talking on the phone to my great-aunt Sophie and reliving the nightmare of the day. I could barely eat; I was so upset. I talked so long that my cell phone died.

I can't go anywhere without my phone. What if my baby needs me? What if there is another emergency at home?

I stopped home and put the phone on the charger and planned to leave immediately. This turned out to be a mistake because the baby needed to eat and I decided to nurse her. When I was done, I was too tired to go back out again.

I decided to spend the night alone on the futon in the basement, and despite my engorged breasts, I knew I needed to sleep and let my husband supplement for a night.

In the middle of the night I woke up in a panic. I called my mom, dad, and husband from the basement to discuss how I *poisoned* my son, even though the nurse had reassured me earlier that day that I gave the correct dosages of medication.

My parents told me not to call them in the middle of the night again and that I was being irrational.

I felt like I had no one to turn to—no one could understand what I experienced—hell, I didn't even know how to explain it because I didn't understand it myself.

My mother-in-law, Sylvia, was coming from Iowa the next day to stay with us for a while. She planned to play with the boys and make us some meals. I called to warn grandma what she was getting herself into. It would be no vacation at our house.

Brace yourself, Sylvia, you're about to enter hell!

Thursday, October 22, 2009

When Sylvia arrived that afternoon I was nervous and on edge. She made herself at home cooking meals for the family, while I anxiously paced the room. I couldn't sit still and I couldn't relax. The wave of dizziness came back, and I felt like I was outside of my body. The one night of rest helped a little bit, but I was still fatigued beyond belief. I was embarrassed to have my mother-in-law see our family in such disarray.

When Sylvia served up a great home-cooked meal that night, I couldn't sit down to eat it. I had completely lost the ability to concentrate on even the simplest tasks, including sitting still long enough to eat a meal.

I sequestered myself down to the basement again and tried to sleep, but it was impossible. It felt like my body was both overcaffeinated and drunk at the same time and that the fatigue and anxiety were fighting each other like two soldiers at war.

I was terrified the most by not understanding what was happening to my body and not being able to explain how awful I felt to anyone.

CHAPTER 7

OB/GYN Visit

Friday, October 23, 2009

I shouldn't get behind the wheel. I can barely stand up. Something is very wrong with me. I need to get help right away.

My four-year-old son had preschool that morning and I was terrified to drive him because of my dizziness. However, it was the beginning of the year and he had already missed quite a few days of school due to the birth of the baby, so I was determined for him to go.

My mother-in-law didn't want to drive him because she was unfamiliar with the roads. I made the decision that it was only a ten-mile drive and I could handle it. Besides, I was finally going to my gynecologist to discuss the possibility that I may have postpartum depression, and I didn't want to miss the appointment.

When I drove to the preschool, I felt like I was floating and was sure I was going to fall asleep at the wheel. I was shocked that the cops didn't pull me over.

In retrospect, I should have never gotten in the car. I managed to get my son to school in one piece, but looking around his classroom everything seemed blurry and surreal.

I started questioning where I was and what I was doing. I felt like I was in a strange dreamland. No one at the preschool noticed my disorientation, so the chaos I was feeling in the inside wasn't that apparent on the outside.

I drove about ten more miles to my doctor's office. The nurse asked me to get on the scale, and as soon as I stood up, I felt the room spinning and

I started to fall over. Several staff members hurdled together and caught me. Then they called for additional help to carry me into an examining room.

There was a new young doctor there that day that I hadn't seen before. When she came into the room, I was really ashamed about what had just happened. I didn't want to be the patient that everyone discussed at their weekly meeting. I was afraid she would think I'm an unfit mother, but she just looked really concerned.

I was clearly unable to stand up on my own, and because of this, she sent me to the emergency room for more testing. She wanted to make sure that the dizziness wasn't a sign of a serious neurologic condition.

I was so embarrassed by my scene and felt like all of the pregnant women in the waiting room were staring at me. They probably wondered why this crazy woman was being whisked away. I had been coming to this clinic throughout my pregnancy and I was always *normal*.

What is happening to me?

I didn't see my friend Regina that day at the clinic, even though she worked there and I was certain she would find out what was going on. I didn't want her to see me this way, and I was ashamed by the scene I had caused at the clinic.

My cell phone was going dead, but I managed to make a quick call to my dad letting him know what was happening. My husband hadn't heard from me and was growing increasingly concerned. He called the clinic and they told him I had been sent to the emergency room, but they couldn't give him any details on my condition due to privacy laws.

Eirik quickly left work and when he arrived, he found me at the hospital in the ER bed. He called my parents to give them an update, but my dad was already on his way to the hospital. Eirik was really disappointed that I had called my dad before him. I tried to call him too but didn't leave a message, because I didn't want to waste my phone's battery.

When my dad arrived, he walked into the hospital emergency room where they checked me out and was immediately distressed and concerned about my condition.

I yelled at him to leave. I told him that someone needed to pick up Evan from preschool—I wanted to make sure he made it home safely. I was more worried about him being stranded at school than about what was happening to me.

Why is everyone so worried about me? How horrible would it be if Evan was left alone at school, his own mother forgetting about him? He would be scarred for life and it would be my fault.

I was given IV fluids at the hospital, thinking I may be dehydrated and this could help with the dizziness. They also prescribed a pill for vertigo and another one for anxiety.

The doctor couldn't find anything clinically wrong with me except for the fact that I had a painful breast infection called mastitis, in which my breasts were red and swollen.

It felt like I was carrying heavy molten rocks on my chest. I'm certain this happened from the one night of sleep I got where I didn't nurse the baby. It figures—I tried for one night of reprieve and ended up with intense pain.

The medication that I was given meant I couldn't breast-feed for twenty-four hours and I had to pump and dump. I didn't like this idea at all because I still wouldn't be able to sleep at night if I had to get up to pump. I've never been able to get the breast pump to work properly and it always frustrated me, and this time was no exception.

They gave me a breast pump in the hospital and I squeezed and squeezed and hardly a drop came out! I felt like an ugly cow with tits of steel. And of course, pumping with mastitis hurt like hell!

I was sent home with the prescriptions and told to try and get some rest. I still didn't believe that I, *Supermom*, could possibly have a mood disorder. I wanted to feel in control of my mind, not like I was losing it. The thought of not being able to control my emotions was worse than any physical ailment, so I kept focusing on the physical feelings I was experiencing.

During the night I was so paranoid that I wouldn't hear Emily's cries and that I would forget to feed her, that I fought the battle of sleep and became even dizzier, more tired, and increasingly confused.

Despite the medication, I started to feel worse. The drunk and anxious collision that was happening in my body was getting stronger all of the time. I became increasingly debilitated and was unable to care for myself, yet alone my kids.

I was petrified of being alone with the children. I didn't feel like I could take care of their basic needs or use sound judgment. I was afraid that the incident with Eithan's medication would happen again and that terrified me. I just wanted to run away and hide because I couldn't stand being a bad mother.

Saturday, October 24, 2009

I hated the way the medication made me feel so groggy and out of it, so the next day I decided that I would be done with the pills.

All day long I anxiously paced back and forth throughout the house. I tried to sleep and the more that I tried to sleep, the less I could. I was becoming increasingly more of an insomniac.

I didn't understand that my body needed time to adjust to the medication. I was so scared about feeling out of control, and I worried that taking medication would affect my judgment even more. I felt myself playing a game of tug-of-war in my mind and I was damned if I did and damned if I didn't.

My husband and his sister were taking the boys to the zoo for a Halloween party that day. I did not feel well enough to go, so I stayed back home with my mother-in-law and the new baby.

I tried to take advantage of the quiet house, but I was so agitated that I couldn't sit still. I paced around all day long. I couldn't concentrate on anything—not even a TV show or reading a magazine. I didn't want to hold my baby for fear that I would drop her. I felt like there was a monster lurking inside my body and I wanted it out—now!

That evening, my mother-in-law drank some wine and I decided to have a drink—perhaps that would numb the pain I was feeling. I hadn't had any alcohol in nine months but thought the wine might take the edge off.

I didn't just sip it like I normally do, I chugged it down in desperation. It worked, and I felt temporarily better. Then I wanted to find pills. I searched the linen closet where we keep the drugs for some type of remedy. I wasn't suicidal; I was just desperate for a cure to my problem.

Luckily, I stopped myself there. I became very frightened that I would take too many pills and overdose because I felt out of control. A few years ago I had a terrible migraine, and I accidentally overdosed on NoDoze, a stimulant that I mistook for Advil. I had a terrible reaction of vomiting, shakiness, and trembling. Eirik was out of town and my parents rushed over to help me because I was alone. I knew I didn't want to experience that day again.

I didn't know what was happening to my body, but I was becoming more ill with each passing day. I was also becoming more and more distant both physically and emotionally with my children, mostly due to my fear of not being able to care for them.

At this point, the baby was sleeping in our room and I got up every hour on the hour to feed her, even if it was a bottle; because Eirik had to work at six in the morning, whereas I was going to be home all day.

I pleaded with my husband to take over the feedings that night because I couldn't handle it anymore; I desperately needed to sleep.

Unfortunately, he was as sleep deprived as I was, and when 2:00 am rolled around, neither one of us was being reasonable.

When the baby wouldn't stop crying, a major fight between Eirik and I broke out about who was going to take care of Emily. I won and he got her, but I was so upset about the fight that I couldn't fall asleep for several hours.

I woke up a few hours later in hysterics. I had seen images of my son Eithan and niece Allie decorating Halloween cookies, but instead of looking cute with black and orange frosting all across their faces, the images became terrifying. Their cute smiles had become devils and the orange and black colors seemed to pop out at me, like they were trying to get me.

The psychiatrist later said this was an indication of hallucination, a sign of psychosis.

While this photo looks like the kids are having fun making Halloween cookies, it is this image that spurred me into a hallucination. When I was sick, the kids looked evil to me.

Sunday, October 25, 2009

The next morning I was even more sleep deprived and anxious than the day before. I knew that I desperately needed help and that I was becoming sicker with each passing hour.

I barely had the energy to do anything, but I mustered up whatever I had left to go through an information packet for new moms from the hospital and found a crisis hotline number.

I called the crisis line and got a man on the other line. I explained how I was feeling out of control, dizzy, fatigued, confused, and paranoid. I told him that I didn't want to take the medications prescribed from the emergency room because I was breast-feeding and pumping and dumping was even more stressful to me.

Unfortunately, the man on the crisis line didn't have any advice and I felt even more helpless and afraid. He said he'd never dealt with a situation like this before. He told me that he didn't know anything about breast-feeding or which type of medications to take or not take.

I asked him if there was anyone else I could call for help, and he said that I could try to contact a doctor on Monday.

I was so upset at this point—even the crisis line didn't know how to help me! I was in a crisis and the crisis line had nothing to say! I didn't know who else to reach out to. I was at my wit's end! I was shocked that they could even call it a crisis line if the crisis workers didn't even know how to deal with callers' problems. I hung up the phone feeling even more hopeless and anxious.

I made it my goal to try and get some sleep. I sequestered myself to the basement for another night and left Eirik and Sylvia in charge of the baby and the boys.

I kept squeezing my breasts nervously, unable to get an ounce of sleep. I squeezed and squeezed, dumping milk all over the sheets, blanket, and carpet. The entire room smelled like rotten milk.

All I wanted to do was sleep, knowing this would cure a lot of my problems. But the more I thought about sleeping, the harder time I had falling asleep.

I once again decided to take the antianxiety medication, even though I knew I would have to pump and dump—something that stressed me out even more.

The entire day I avoided my children like the plague. I absolutely couldn't handle their demands, especially since I couldn't even take care of myself.

I begged Eirik to go to Target to buy me a handheld breast pump since I was too disoriented to drive myself. I thought that might be easier to use than the fancy electric one. He said he was busy with the kids and couldn't go for a while, and I became even more agitated. I hated relying on other people. When I want something, I want it *now*!

I went up to our bedroom and tried to sleep again but couldn't.

Please God, let me sleep! I don't care about anything else anymore.

I then started pacing around the room, repeating over and over, "Help me. Help me. Help me," but no one really listened.

I started crying for Eirik to come, but he was still really busy taking care of all three kids and the boys were becoming afraid of what happened to their mother.

"Please, you've got to help me!" I begged.

"What do you need?" he asked.

"I just need you to hold me. I am so scared. Please hold me and never let me go," I cried.

He finally came upstairs, letting his mom take over the kids, which was a difficult thing for him to do, and I hung on to him like he was my life support and if I let go I would die.

We cuddled on the bed for a while and it made me feel a little safer. We decided to take a shower together. He thought that may help me to relax as well as get rid of the rotten milk smell.

I just held him close, closed my eyes, and tried to imagine that everything was okay. But I knew things weren't.

People had no idea what was going on inside of me, and I didn't understand it either. I didn't know where to turn for help. The sicker I got, the more paranoid I became about what was happening to me. I was feeling increasingly desperate and hopeless.

How could it be just a month earlier I was smiling at my newborn daughter imagining all of the fun times we would have?

Now it felt like those dreams were squashed and I was in hell.

Around dinnertime I decided to call my friend Regina.

She said to me, "Stacey, I know of a hospital with a psychiatric unit. Tell them that you insist on staying. You need to get help before this becomes a dangerous situation," she said.

She then called the hospital and insisted that they admit me.

I felt completely relieved that someone was going to do something about my situation. I didn't want to go the hospital, but I knew I *desperately* needed help.

CHAPTER 8

Checking into the Hospital

I can't live this way. I don't even know who I am anymore. If I don't get some sleep soon, I'm going to die.

I will never forget the day I went to the hospital. It was Emily's one-month birthday and I wasn't sure if I'd ever be the same again.

While Eirik and my mom argued over who would drive me to the emergency room, I just stood there staring at them like a deer looking into headlights. I couldn't deal with the family drama.

On the drive there (Eirik ended up taking me), everything seemed a little more normal for a few minutes. I started thinking that going to the hospital was a little ridiculous and that they'd probably send me right home. Maybe I was just imagining all of this. Perhaps the sleep deprivation was getting to me, but I'd be fine. I actually sang a few songs on the radio and felt pretty good. I finally had hope that I would be okay.

The check-in gal immediately asked me if I was suicidal and I said, "No." Since I wasn't an immediate threat to myself, I waited and waited and waited for what seemed like an eternity.

When they finally brought me back to the evaluation area, this was like no part of the hospital I had ever seen. It seemed like I was visiting a high-security prison.

Suddenly I felt like I had done something wrong. I felt like a criminal and was afraid the authorities were going to lock me away for trying to poison my son. I was paranoid of everyone and everything around me. But I wanted to get help—whatever it took.

The area was stark white and not the least bit friendly. It was filled with security guards everywhere. I asked to go to the bathroom, and I had to be escorted there with a guard waiting in front of the door and cameras watching my every move.

Where am I?

We were then put in a small room with a large metal door with guards outside. We were told we couldn't close the door. My husband was asked to leave the room so I could be questioned by a psychiatrist. They put him in a separate room and interrogated him as well.

The psychiatrist opened up a notebook to record our conversation then asked me if I was going to hurt myself or the baby. I had no intention of either. I just wanted to get help!

I love my baby girl more than anything in the world, but I didn't trust my competency around my children. I was physically unstable and could barely take care of myself, yet alone three small kids.

At the ER, I was also given a drug test. I didn't realize this was being done. Had I known at the time, I would have likely become even more paranoid that I was being judged as an unfit mother.

I still don't know exactly what they asked Eirik, but I'm pretty sure they were trying to find out if I was a threat to myself or the baby. I was really worried that the authorities would think I was insane and that they would lock me up for life.

I really didn't care what was going to happen next. I just wanted sleeping pills to get rid of this nightmare and to wake up the next morning feeling great and to go home to life as normal.

It was getting really late and I told Eirik to get back home to the kids. I told him I'd call him in the morning when it was time to come home. I was given some heavy-duty drugs for sleeping and I passed out on the emergency room bed. I remember opening my eyes every few hours and wondering where I was and what was happening, but I was too exhausted to really care.

CHAPTER 9

The First Twenty-Four Hours

Monday, October 26, 2009

When I woke up the next morning, I felt much better rested than I had in weeks. I would have slept in a garbage can if it meant I could get a few hours of shut-eye.

I pondered what I would do that morning. I was so thankful to have finally gotten a good night's sleep that I didn't care where I was. There was no crying baby or whining kids. While this definitely wasn't the Embassy Suites, I was trying to make the most out of my quiet morning.

That's when it really occurred to me that this wasn't the *regular* hospital. The walls were all white, the doors were heavy, and there was nothing in the room. There was no phone, no TV, no window.

Am I dreaming? Am I in hell? Where is all of my stuff?

Then a staff worker came out with a lock box and showed me all of my belongings. They had confiscated any clothes with strings, my shoes, my purse, and my Blackberry (gasp—that was my lifeline)! I was completely cut off from the outside world. I was wearing turquoise scrubs that were about three sizes too big.

I asked to take a shower and was led by lock and key through a heavy metal door. There was no running water. I was told to speak into the intercom when I was ready and they'd turn on the water. Apparently running water was a safety hazard.

I called my husband that morning from a hospital phone that was being monitored by staff. They listened to every word of my conversation.

I was feeling pretty good at the time and assumed that I was just sleep deprived, and after a good night's sleep I would be ready to go. Eirik worked nearby and said he could pick me up during lunch or on his way home. Neither one of us expected this nightmare to continue as long as it did.

The hospital staff had me sign a release allowing nurses to answer questions about my condition. I put my husband, mom, dad, and Regina on the list. I'm sure glad that I did or they would have been really worried once I was no longer able to communicate with anyone.

I didn't realize until recently that my husband and parents were communicating with the nurses because I was so out of it, but they spoke to them several times a day for updates on my condition.

I paced around all day not sure quite what to do with my time. I spent most of it making phone calls to my mom, dad, and husband. I then learned that I was in a holding area for twenty-four hours to evaluate my condition. I suddenly became scared of my surroundings.

Who are these people in the other cells? Am I in a safe place? I don't belong here! I'm not going to harm myself or anyone else.

That morning I was deemed *safe* and clear to move over to the step-down unit, a transitional place for people after they pass the observation period, but they didn't have any available rooms.

While in my solitary confinement area that day I had three visitors: my OB/GYN doctor who I had seen during my pregnancy, Dr. Anderson, a student social worker, and a psychiatrist. Each asked me very detailed questions about my condition and took thorough notes.

When Dr. Anderson came to visit, I was totally embarrassed to let him see me this way. After all, I had come to his office several times throughout the pregnancy and was a perfectly *normal* person. Now I was afraid he would think I was a crazy person who was locked up in a mental health institution.

I think he was a little taken aback by my condition. He was an older man who had seen many things in his practice, but I felt like he'd never seen someone change so drastically.

His mannerism was very calm and professional and he didn't seem surprised at all by my condition, yet I still worried about what he thought of me. I asked him if he'd seen other patients here before.

"Yes, I have," he said.

I thought he was lying. *No one could be as fucked up as me!*

The second visitor was a young student social worker who was there doing an internship. She asked me to recall all of the major events leading up to how I came to the hospital. She also questioned things like my overall happiness in my life, marriage, and childhood. I thought this was ridiculous—I love my life. I've always been very happy. I wanted my life back, not to escape it.

That's also when I met my psychiatrist, Dr. Wilson, for the first time. He was a middle-aged tall and heavyset man whose shirt was hanging out of his pants. He was the no-bullshit type—just get to the point and move along. There was no easing you into your diagnosis. It was like he was hitting a baseball and whacked you right in the face with it.

He instantly had me pegged. "I know your type," he said. "You're *Supermom*. You try and do it all."

I was a bit offended that after knowing me for an hour he could characterize my personality. I just wanted to know what the hell was wrong with me.

He described my condition as "The cup was full and it tipped. When you're on top you have further to fall," he said.

I didn't think of myself as a *Supermom* ever before, but if you ask my friends and family they will say I'm a "supercharged Type A personality."

For me being busy and taking on a lot of projects is just normal—I've always thought of this as a positive quality that has brought me a lot of success in life.

I didn't disagree with his statement, but it seemed pretty surreal that my strongest qualities would also be my weakest link.

Will the supercharged Stacey ever come back? I like that Stacey a lot better than this paranoid one!

Dr. Wilson's notes from that first psychological profiling read as follows:

Ms. Ackerman is a thirty-five-year-old married Caucasian female. This is her first psychiatric hospitalization. She appears to be having a psychotic depression postpartum. She also endorses all the symptoms of panic attacks with abrupt onset of multiple physical symptoms of feeling light-headed, anxious, chest was hurting, heart racing, and shortness of breath. She has a sense of derealization and depersonalization. She has numbness, tingling, nausea. She has never had mental health treatment. She has a great deal of denial about having mental health issues to begin with. She was not sleeping, feeding the baby every hour on the hour. Patient continues to be extremely sleep deprived.

CHAPTER 10

Moving to the Step-Down Unit

I had a good night's sleep. I feel better. Now I need to get the hell out of here and get back to my kids.

It was getting later in the day and I was still wondering when I was going to go home.

I asked one of the employees and he said, "You're going to need to stay for a few days."

"What!" I screamed. "Are you kidding me? Why do I need to stay here? I got a great night of sleep and I feel a zillion times better."

I called Eirik to let him know not to pick me up that day. Then I got really concerned about the kids.

"Did you know that Evan has a parents' day at school tomorrow? And on Tuesday the boys have music class," I continued.

Oh my God, how is he going to get them where they need to be? I'm the one who always schedules all of their activities. He doesn't even know what's going on this week. What about all of Eithan's medications? He may not know when to give him his meds. What if he gets sicker?

I was afraid that the family would not be able to function without me.

Later that afternoon, I got to visit the step-down unit. It was very different from the other side. There were people everywhere and there was no privacy. I felt overwhelmed by all of the activity, even though I'm normally a very social person. After coming from solitary confinement and days alone in my basement, this place seemed a little chaotic. There were activity charts and people gathering together. It was a complete culture shock to go from one environment to the next. It was like I entered another world. Besides pointing out an activity calendar, no one explained what was going on or what was expected of me. I really needed this even more than normal because I was so confused.

I decided to grab a chair and join a discussion group that was already in progress. A pharmacist was there talking about medications. People were asking a lot of questions and they all seemed to be familiar with these medication names. I'd never heard of any of them. Besides an occasional allergy medication or antibiotic, I'd never even taken medications in my entire thirty-five years.

I looked around the room eyeing the other patients one by one. I tried to figure out why these people were so crazy. I felt badly for them, but definitely didn't consider myself to be *one of them*.

It's funny, but the sicker I got, the more *normal* they all became. At first I thought everyone was crazy but me, and then I thought I was the only one who was crazy.

I noticed a middle-aged man crossing his legs and twitching his body. He seemed scruffy and had funny-looking teeth. I figured he must be a person that is frequently institutionalized.

I later learned, much to my dismay, that he was a suburban dad who lived near me and that this was his first hospitalization too.

It's funny how easy it is to judge people without really knowing their story.

There was also a pregnant woman there. I was afraid to look at her because it reminded me of the baby I had that was home without me. I never heard this woman talk or learned her name or her story. She would lie on the couch in the fetal position, crying and rocking. During the rest of my stay, she was sent to solitary confinement.

I decided to check the rest of the place out. It reminded me a lot of when I used to work in a nursing home. It smelled like shit and reeked of death and illness. I hated that nursing home. They used to count bodies in the morning to see how we were doing on our *sales* goals. People weren't treated as people; they were treated as bed numbers. It was an awful job seeing people living out the end of their lives in such a terrible place.

I felt very alone in the psychiatric unit and scared out of my wits. I looked around. Not much there. There was a long narrow hall with worn-out blue carpet and wooden hand rails. The area where the group was taking place was also used for eating, watching TV, or reading. There was an old phone in the hallway that looked like a pay phone but didn't require any quarters. Of course, the line was monitored by staff so there was absolutely no privacy. There was an occupational therapy room where people could do art projects at certain times of the day.

Art projects, really? Am I in kindergarten?

While visiting the occupational therapy room, a heavyset woman in her late thirties, with short blond hair, fell off of a stool and started having a seizure. I've always been terrified of hospitals and anything medical, so it really scared me. I should have tried to help, but I just sat there dumbfounded.

A few hours later, one of the psychiatric assistants said they were moving me to the step-down unit.

"Come on, we want you to meet your new roommate," he said.

I hesitantly entered the room. It was right across from the nurses' station. It had grayish-white linoleum floors and two hospital beds with handrails. There were a few pictures on the wall, but I can't recall what they were of. There was a tiny bathroom but no mirror because some patients may try and harm themselves with the glass. There was a large window that faced down to the main entrance of the hospital, and there was some construction taking place outside. There was a windowsill to sit on, but the window didn't open at all.

When I saw who my roommate was I got a little nervous. She was the woman who just had the seizure.

The first thing she said to me was, "I'm so sorry."

"For what?" I asked.

"For falling over in OT." she said.

"You can't help that," I replied.

I then asked her what her name was and why she was here.

"I'm Cherise, and I'm suicidal," she said matter-of-factly.

I had never met anyone before that was suicidal—at least no one who's ever admitted it. I was worried that she would want me to help her kill herself.

I was really afraid of her at first. I felt like a terrified grade school child in this new environment. I was out of place and not sure what to do or how to act. I suddenly became very fearful of the other residents. There are men here, I thought. I don't know what these people are capable of doing. I worried about my safety.

I'm normally a very trusting person and believe people are inherently good, but I was too anxious to see the good in these strangers.

We're all on this enclosed floor together. How do I know these people are safe?

I asked one of the nurses if I was going to be safe and she assured me I would.

Then one of the other residents told me, "Everyone here is pretty nice, you just have to watch out for that guy," and he pointed to a big angry-looking man.

Apparently a fight had broken out between him and one of the other residents.

Holy shit, a fight!

This was so different than my suburban mom lifestyle. I desperately wanted to go home.

That night I tried to get to sleep and couldn't, even though I was so horribly sleep deprived.

My brother, who served in Afghanistan, says that sleep deprivation is one of the worst forms of torture, and I can believe it.

I was barely functioning at this point. I was terrified of where I was. I was certain that this was just a nightmare and soon I'd wake up in my bed and see my smiling husband's face and rock my baby to sleep.

I would periodically open my eyes and look around the room then freak out about my surroundings. I was convinced that I had *gone crazy* and would be institutionalized for the rest of my life.

I started fearing for my kids' lives. I had abandoned them. They were all going to suffer. I had the irrational fear that my kids wouldn't survive without me, even though Eirik is a very capable dad. I believed that I would never be given the opportunity to raise Emily. I felt like she wasn't really my baby, that this whole giving birth thing was another life a long time ago.

The physical ailments I had experienced at home started to get much, much more intense. When I lied down, I felt a shooting sensation that went from my toes up to my legs and spine and into my head like a zip line. Something was moving inside of me, but I was lying still. It felt similar to an adrenaline rush that you get when you ride a roller coaster.

I later learned that these physical sensations were signs of panic, but at the time, I was convinced that I was suffering from a serious neurological disorder. I demanded an MRI, but no one would order one.

I held ice packs to my swollen breasts and started screaming, "Where is my baby? I need to feed her!"

I ran out to the nurses' station and pleaded for help. I told them I couldn't sleep and that something awful was going to happen to my kids. I didn't feel safe at all.

I decided to spend the night in the hallway where I could see the nurses. At least there were some *normal* people that could keep me safe from the *crazies*. I was convinced that I was never going to make it out of this horrible hell.

CHAPTER 11

Getting Sicker

I had made a conscious decision that I would block my family out of my mind. If they didn't exist, then the pain of the separation wouldn't be as difficult.

I decided that my main focus needed to be myself and my healing and that I couldn't worry about anyone else. As a mother, I spend most of my time taking care of other people. This was my chance to focus on me.

That morning I met with Dr. Wilson, the psychiatrist who had visited me the previous day. He prescribed an antianxiety medication, an antidepressant and some heavy-duty sleeping pills.

"You really need sleep," he said. "This will help."

That night I became terrified out of my wits again. I kept the bathroom light on because I was afraid of the dark. I started screaming in terror in the middle of the night.

Cherise was so nice and understanding and assured me that it didn't bother her. I am usually very chatty, but I couldn't even hold a conversation with Cherise.

In the middle of the night, I got up and went to the nurses' station. I needed help. I was afraid. I didn't know what had taken over my body. As I walked toward the nurses' station, I collapsed on the ground in a big heap.

A hospital doctor was paged and within minutes came to examine me. He couldn't find anything physically wrong with me. I was convinced that I was in hell and was going to die in this hospital. My incident was put in the nurse's notes and given to the psychiatrist in the morning.

The next day I felt really confused.

Where am I and what am I doing here? Is this all just a bad dream? It sure feels like a nightmare!

The nurse came and gave me pills. These pills were supposed to be making me feel better, so why was I feeling so much worse? I couldn't think clearly. I became paranoid that the medications they were giving me were all part of a conspiracy to keep me sedated and confused.

I wasn't quite sure where I was and what I was doing. The constant conflict of sped-up and slowed-down that my body experienced—like a collision of caffeine and alcohol—grew so strong that I thought my body was going to explode.

Suddenly, all of the thoughts inside my head started racing. They were running through my brain like it was on speed. My life kept moving at record pace in my head and I couldn't run fast enough to keep up with it.

I tried to watch TV, but I couldn't focus. It was just words that were coming at me, attacking me. The picture was a blur. It was as if someone had been hitting the fast-forward button.

I tried to read a magazine. This is something I always do at home to relax and unwind. It was as if the words were jumping out of the page and trying to eat me alive.

Nothing was clear. It was all a strange world. It was like I forgot to put my glasses on and all of these images were running by.

I wanted to understand what was happening to my body. My sessions with the psychiatrist flew by so quickly and it seemed like all we talked about were the medications I was taking.

I was upset that no one could explain what was wrong with me. I was hoping there would be a therapist who could tell me what was going on inside my mind. I needed answers, but I wasn't getting any.

Having individualized counseling would have been extremely beneficial, but unfortunately it is a rarity in hospitals today.

That night I decided to refuse medications. I was so uncertain about what was going on and I figured the medications were making me that way. The only thing I knew was that I was worse than when I came in.

The next day, I hit rock bottom. When I met with Dr. Wilson that morning, I hounded him.

"You're drugging me!" I shouted. "How do I even know what you're giving me? These nurses are making me pop pills all day long. I don't even know what I'm taking! I'm feeling worse."

"If you want to get better then you'll let me treat you," he said. "If not, you can leave now. No one is making you stay."

I thought about what could happen if I went home. It would be worse for my kids to have me home and to be out of control. I was determined to get better.

I decided to put my faith in Dr. Wilson and his medications, even though I felt like I had lost the ability to trust anyone. I had come voluntarily and I didn't want to leave the hospital until I felt able to take care of myself and my kids.

I remember Dr. Wilson asking me at our first visit about my family history. My grandfather had bipolar disorder and spent a lot of his adult years in and out of mental health units, often for months at a time. My grandma married him not knowing about his illness—the family had hid it from her. After twenty-some years of marriage, they divorced.

My grandpa also had two siblings with the same illness, one of which was his twin brother, and another who had committed suicide years before I was born.

I feared that my life would mimic his, even though I had led a normal, successful life up until this point. Dr. Wilson told me that a family history of mental illness could be an indicator that I would have a lifelong problem.

I felt hopeless as if my life had been taken away, and I was now somebody else. I didn't think I would ever fully recover. I was certain that my husband would be a single dad of three kids until he found a new *Supermom* that he would marry and replace me with.

That afternoon, Regina came for a visit. She was able to see me during nonvisiting hours because she was on staff at the hospital. When she looked at me I wasn't sure if she was terrified, about to cry, or both. She's always a person of great composure, but I could tell that seeing me in this state was difficult.

"I think you're going to be here a while, Stacey. I have seen a lot of patients with postpartum depression, but this is something more. There is a possibility that you are experiencing postpartum psychosis," she said.

Months later, she described me during this encounter as "unresponsive" and "virtually comatose."

In my delusional state, I was terrified that I had lost my mind. And as a person always in control, I feared that I'd never have control of my emotions again. I was convinced that I was psychotic and was going to live the rest of my life institutionalized.

My dreams of having a daughter are gone. She will never know her real mother. She'll be raised without me, only visiting me occasionally in my delusional state.

These thoughts made my heart feel like it was going through the paper shredder.

I begged the nurses to give me more knowledge on what happened. I felt like I was the only one who was going through this hell.

They printed me of a definition of postpartum depression. "You feel weepy. You cry all of the time. You don't connect with your baby," it said.

This was all fine and well for some people, but this wasn't what happened to me! I didn't feel *those* things. I felt dizzy, confused, out of control, and paranoid, especially of what was happening to me.

I wanted more information. I didn't have access to any resources. I wished there was someone in the hospital who could relate to my condition, but I seemed to be either lumped in with chronically-depressed patients or the classic crying, weeping new mom, of which I was neither.

I rationalized that I must have a physical problem because in talking with the other residents, none of them were experiencing the physical sensations like I was.

I marched up to the nurses' station and told Nurse Connie that I needed to see a neurologist right away—it was an emergency!

She told me that she couldn't do anything and that I'd have to wait until the next morning when I met with Dr. Wilson.

I was so mad! I wanted help now —I couldn't wait!

When I met the next morning with the doc he assured me that there was nothing physically wrong with me. He said that the physical symptoms I felt were real, but they were caused by anxiety. That didn't seem like a good enough medical explanation to me. I wanted more answers. I didn't understand how a psychological problem could transpose into a physical one.

Dr. Wilson explained that with anxiety, the mind triggers a fight or flight response in the body as a protective mechanism when the body senses that it is in danger.

As a result, I experienced physical symptoms, such as rapid heart rate, shakiness, and an out-of-body sensation. I now realize that anxiety and panic can be a physical as well as an emotional disease.

It had been almost a week and I hadn't talked to anyone from the outside world except Regina. Talking to my family at the time was too painful, and I was afraid it would bring on another panic attack.

When I was first admitted to the hospital and had to stop breast-feeding, the nurse on duty consulted with a lactation specialist who told me to stop pumping and let my milk dry up.

My breasts were now the size of basketballs, and they were as hard as them too. I walked around in my turquoise scrubs all day with an ice pack in my bra, and I hadn't showered for days. My breasts were so inflamed and painful, but it was the only reminder I had that I was a new mom.

The simplest, most basic task, such as taking a shower was impossible, because my body was paralyzed by my illness.

I really wanted to take a shower. I was thinking about it all day, but for some reason I couldn't get myself physically there. Every step I took became painful. The room spun. I couldn't remember how to take a shower. All day long I tried to figure out how to take a shower, but I never made it there.

That evening I told one of the nurses about my desire to take a shower. She said she had worked in this hospital for thirty years and had seen many postpartum anxiety patients like me, but I didn't really believe her.

I asked her over and over if I was going to be okay and she said I would. I still couldn't get myself to have faith that I would be alright. I was skeptical about everything.

She said she would take me out and give me a shower. There was a nice spa shower outside of the ward and she would let me out to go there. It was the kindest thing I'd ever heard before. I still can't believe I let a stranger give me a shower, but it felt really good.

The sensations of the water, however, affected me more than normal. When it was hot, it felt burning, and when I got out I was so cold that I shook. The nurse had to hold me up so I wouldn't collapse on the floor. I felt shaky, weak, and trembling.

I kept looking for this nurse again later, wanting to thank her for her kindness. I don't know if I just forgot what she looked like or she really never came back, but she was an angel.

Later that week when I told Dr. Wilson I was unable to take a shower, he said to me, "Look at you. You aren't dirty or unkempt; you are out of bed, wearing clothes."

When Regina spoke to Dr. Wilson, he explained that this was a form of cognitive therapy, a way to show me the disconnection between what

I believed at the time and what was real. As much as I believed that I couldn't take a shower, this wasn't reality. This was a part of my illness.

Being that my condition was getting so much worse, I finally accepted the fact that I wasn't going home anytime soon. I really wanted my own clothes to wear, which were allowed in the step-down unit as long as there were no strings or ties. I was tired of wearing the same few things.

One of the psychiatric assistants suggested I write a list and she'd call a family member to pick up my stuff. She gave me a notebook. I spent all day staring at the notebook trying to remember what I needed and wrote it down.

I was a journalism major in college, so writing normally comes very naturally to me. After about eight hours of trying, I finally wrote the list and here's what it read:

Sweatshirt
Cotton pants – no string – medium
White socks
Sweatpants – no string
Long sleeve shirt

That was about as far as I could get, and that in and of itself was a huge struggle. I wasn't able to make a phone call myself so she called my mom to bring me my belongings.

All the people that I thought were crazy at first I decided were completely normal and that I was the crazy one. I kept asking patients over and over if they thought I was crazy.

The man who I met at the first meeting whose name was Joe, the suburban dad, said to me, "If you were really crazy, you wouldn't be asking if you were crazy. Look at that lady over there, now she's crazy!" he said.

I looked over and saw a woman mumbling out loud and then ranting to herself. Okay, she was a bit crazier than me.

CHAPTER 12

Halloween

Saturday, October 31, 2009

I used to love Halloween. Playing dress up was one of my favorite things to do as a kid, and on Halloween, even grown-ups can get away with playing dress up!

Several Halloweens ago, before Eirik and I had kids, he dressed up as Sammy Hagar and I dressed up as Cher. We had the best time opening the door for all the neighborhood kids, who were somewhat surprised at the grown-ups with the elaborate costumes on.

Being in the hospital for Halloween was really difficult for me.

When I was in the hospital, I met this great woman, Cara, a new patient who also had young kids. She had been hospitalized after the birth of her daughter, so she was one of the few people who seemed to understand my pain.

My friend Cara was getting a pass to go home to see her kids for Halloween, but I knew I wasn't ready to do that yet. I still felt really unstable emotionally and was afraid that seeing my family would cause me another major setback.

Halloween made me realize how much I was missing in their lives and how Eirik was doing his best to keep things as normal as possible at home.

Evan dressed as Scooby Doo and Eithan was a monkey. I had even purchased a costume made for small dogs for Emily, since she was too tiny to wear a kid's costume. It was a pink princess outfit complete with a satin hat and silver glitter.

I remember them trying on their costumes for me a few weeks earlier, while I sat in a chair spaced out, holding Emily in my arms. They were so excited to wear their costumes and to get candy.

I felt like such a worthless parent not being able to spend Halloween with my kids. Halloween is a major milestone in a child's life. As adults, we remember those important milestones from our childhood, like what we wore on the first day of school, what theme we had for our birthday party, and what we dressed up as on Halloween.

Growing up, I'll never forget the Kraft Mac 'n Cheese dinners and hot chocolate my mom would make us before we went out trick-or-treating. Then my brother and I would come home and inventory our candy.

"I got fourteen Snickers," I'd say. "How many did you get?"

Now, in its truest form of irony, this evening will always be kind of spooky in my mind.

Eirik's sister Penny came over to our house to pass out Halloween candy to the neighbor kids. Did people even notice that it wasn't me at the door? A lot of the neighbors didn't even realize I had been gone. We have a close-knit community in our neighborhood, and everyone usually knows what people are up to, but my family was being secretive about my condition, not wanting to embarrass me or the family reputation.

Eirik and the boys went trick-or-treating with friends from the neighborhood. Eirik did his best to give the boys a fun time during this very scary part of our lives.

Tara, a neighbor who saw Eirik that night, later told me that he looked great; no one could tell from the outside how emotionally wrecked he was, but I knew. Unfortunately no one noticed his problems because the focus was on me. Like most men, Eirik is very good at repressing his feelings.

Cara got back in the early evening and we sat on the couch and cried together. While she got to see her kids for a little while, it was still painful for her to go home and then to know she had to come back to the hospital.

There was a big window that I could look out from the couch in the lounge. I tried to picture my kids trick-or-treating at that moment. Then I quickly tried to block out that image because the thoughts were just too painful to deal with.

One of the nurses gave me a journal and said I should start writing things down to remember them. I thought this was a great idea since I love to write. Maybe my mind would work better this way. From then on, I wrote everything down.

That evening my journal entry went like this:

God is watching over us.
God will take care of us.
There's only up.
I will survive.
God is testing my strength.
I will get by.
Don't worry, be happy.
One day I'll look back on this and it won't seem like a big deal.
I've lived many other days and have been just fine.
I have a great support system.
Just one moment at a time.
Just breathe.
Just breathe.
I'm okay.
I'm okay.
I am in control.
I am going to take small steps to get better.

While I was born and raised Jewish, I've never been an overly spiritual person. During this time, however, I decided to put my faith in God—after all, that's all I had left. I couldn't reason or rationalize this condition like I do with most other elements of my life.

CHAPTER 13

Am I Ever Going to Leave?

Breakfast? Is it time for breakfast now? Did I order breakfast? How do I order breakfast? Where are the forms? Where are the pencils? How do I draw a circle?

Every morning, the residents were supposed to take an order form and order their meals for the day. I had been there for a week before I even realized this. Then, when I went to try and circle my meal selection on the paper menu, it was difficult. I couldn't remember how to do it. The colored pencil shook in my hand. I couldn't read the words. My two-year-old could have figured this out, yet I was struggling to complete a very simple task. I saw new residents coming in all of the time and ordering meals without any trouble. What was wrong with me?

Then one day I realized there was a daily schedule of where we were supposed to be. I don't know what I'd been doing all week, but I certainly wasn't at group or following any type of schedule. Besides briefly showing me the calendar the first day, no one ever encouraged me to go to the group sessions. If I sat in my room all day, no one really said anything about it. Not following a schedule or going where other people are was very atypical for me.

I decided to make an effort to try and go to the group meetings. I asked Cherise if she would watch over me and tell me what time it was and where to go since I couldn't seem to remember on my own. She said she would do that.

I felt so grateful to have someone to look out for me. I'm normally very independent and don't like to rely on other people, but I needed to know someone was watching my back because I couldn't trust my thoughts or actions.

At this time, I became aware that we were supposed to go up to the nurses' station at certain times of the day and ask for our meds. The entire time the nurses tracked me down and handed me my prescriptions. I thought they did this to everyone.

What a strange irony that as someone who thrives on a schedule and routine, I couldn't get the hang of the schedule or routine at the hospital to save my life.

Finally, I went up and asked for the meds on my own. I felt so proud of myself for the recent realization of the world around me.

"Do you know what medicine you're supposed to take Stacey?" the nurse asked.

They were changing my dosages and prescriptions almost daily, trying to get the right combination—I'm not sure if I would be able to keep up with it in my usual state of mind.

"I have no idea," I said, "but I came up here today on my own."

It felt like the nurse was being condescending to me as though I was a child. I was just happy that I was developing more awareness of my surroundings, which was a major breakthrough.

I was constantly looking for reassurance that I'd get better. I still wasn't convinced I was ever going to lead a normal life again. I constantly hung out at the nurses' station asking a million questions and wanting someone to tell me that I was going to be okay.

I also wanted information and facts. I didn't understand this illness. It wasn't logical to me that I could be sick in my head, when I felt it so much in my body.

I still thought I was going to end up like Winona Ryder in the movie *Girl Interrupted*, where a high school girl is sent to live in a mental institution.

During my sessions with the doctor, we mostly discussed my medications. I was frustrated that I wasn't gaining any more understanding of my disease from him. I wanted to know why this happened to me, and when and how I was going to get better.

I attended the group sessions hoping to find answers, but they never seemed to address my specific condition. I wanted to learn about postpartum mood disorders, but the groups were more focused on other conditions, as I was the only patient who was postpartum. I didn't find this helpful at all.

That day when I met with Dr. Wilson, he took out his medical textbook and read me off the definition of panic disorder.

Feeling like you're going crazy; a fear of dying, a physical sensation running through your body; dizziness; memory loss and confusion; paranoia.

This textbook definition made me feel a million times better. It was so nice to know that the weirdness I was feeling was an actual condition and that I wasn't really crazy. It validated what I had been feeling this entire time.

He made me a photocopy of this definition and I carried it around with me everywhere like a little pet. This piece of paper made me feel grounded. It was the only bit of reassurance I had that I wasn't insane.

That day I wrote in my journal:

God, give me the strength to overcome this.
To give peace to me and my family.
Tonight I will rest and realize that some things I cannot control.
But tomorrow will be a brighter day.
Find trust in those trying to heal me.

While I had been too self-absorbed until this point to get to know the other residents, I finally reached out to my roommate. It was weird that we shared a room for so long but hardly knew each other. For a brief moment in time I was myself, and I was able to engage in a conversation. She told me she had visions of killing herself and couldn't get them out of her mind. She had been at this hospital just a few weeks earlier and was back again. It was really nice to feel like I had a friend to confide in.

We hung out in our room for a while and giggled like two school girls at a slumber party. It was such a nice moment. Then we both sat up on the windowsill and talked about our lives in the outside world.

"You really should meet me some other time. I'd like to introduce you to the real me," I said.

For a brief moment in time, my witty sense of humor came back.

She told me about her job at Joann Fabrics and how she loved to sew and knit. She knit a baby blanket during her stay that she would donate to a crisis nursery. I had a hard time looking at the baby blanket, because it reminded me of the baby I missed.

Cherise was a very spiritual person and had her priest come visit and pray for her several times during her stay.

Unlike me who was worried about going back to a large family with a ton of responsibility, she was worried about going home and being alone.

I felt really sorry for her. How lonely it must be not to have a family. It made me appreciate my family so much, but thinking about them made my heart feel like it was being torn apart, so I quickly shut out the thought.

I called Cherise once after I got home, when she was in a halfway house. At first she didn't remember who I was. I still have her phone number programmed into my cell phone. I often think about trying to reach out to her, but I am so afraid that I will learn she didn't have a happy ending, and I'm not sure I'm emotionally ready to handle news like that.

Unfortunately, my period of clarity didn't last more than a few hours. It became increasingly difficult to talk to people. There was just too much *noise*. The only way I could really have a conversation with anyone was by being in a quiet room, looking the other person in the eye and trying my best to focus. Any stimulus from other sources was like a soda with fizz spilling over the top—my brain just couldn't take any excess information.

What went from anxiety started to turn to hopelessness and depression. I didn't come to the hospital depressed, but the longer I was away from my family, the more hopeless and depressed I felt.

I was afraid that this was my new life. I started thinking about my baby and got really sad. I was afraid she wasn't going to remember me and that I wasn't going to remember her.

I curled myself into a fetal position and sobbed. I refused to come out to eat or meet during group time. I just wanted to be alone. Me, the social butterfly, alone? This was so out of character, but it was too unbearable to face my life this way.

I found one of the psychiatric assistants, the woman that helped me write the list and I asked her, "Am I going to get better? Please tell me I'm going to get better."

"We don't like to keep people here forever," she said. "I've worked here for many years, and I've never seen someone not leave," she said.

That gave me some added reassurance. After all, it seemed very logical, and I was dying to grab onto some piece of logic in this crazy mixed-up nightmare I was having.

"We've had many patients here with postpartum mood disorders and they've all turned out okay," she reassured me. "Why don't you write in your notebook?" she said.

And suddenly I did my best to be strong and find hope that I would make it through this difficult time. Writing kept me grounded. And here's what I wrote:

I will be okay.
I am a good mother.
I can cope.
I am going to take care of myself so I can take care of my kids.
I am not crazy.
There will be brighter days ahead.
We're the Ackermans and we can make it through anything.
Stay strong.
Stay strong.
Stay strong.
I can do it.
I can get through the next five minutes; just worry about that.
I have the power within me to heal.

I still wasn't sure I completely trusted Dr. Wilson, so I asked Regina to come with me to my next meeting with him. I don't think the doctor was pleased about another medical professional questioning his authority.

Regina is a great friend and even tested the line a little to help me. Afterward, she told me that he really knows his stuff, that he is a competent doctor, and that I should listen to what he has to say. Hearing this gave me the peace of mind I needed to allow myself to fully trust him, because I couldn't rationalize the situation on my own.

Several of the residents who were at the hospital when I arrived were going to be leaving. I was really terrified of this because these people had been so positive and helpful to me when I felt like a scared and alone child.

The residents decided to have a movie and popcorn night. I thought this was such a cool thing to do. Everyone gathered in the lounge in their pajamas and enjoyed a few hours of normalcy.

I couldn't tell you what the movie was, only that it was something on an old VHS tape and it was from the '80s. My concentration was still terrible and I couldn't focus on the movie at all. I just lied down on the floor with a pillow and blanket and let myself finally feel safe in this room full of people that were once complete strangers and were now the only people in my life who understood me.

I think the experience is similar to what army troops go through. These scary, shared experiences bring soldiers together in a unified way that the outside world can't relate to.

I had a real hard time saying goodbye to my new friends. I couldn't even remember most of their names (hell, I'm not sure I could remember my own name), but the way they touched my life was so special.

I began panicking again as suddenly I was one of the people who had been hospitalized the longest—it had been a full week. The average stay is three days.

Why aren't I getting better? Are they going to send me to live in an institution? Am I ever going to leave?

By this time I was well enough to take a shower by myself. I even asked one of the psych assistants if she'd get me my makeup out of my purse which was locked away.

I am not usually someone who goes out in public without makeup on, and I wanted to feel more like myself again. I normally wear contacts, but when we went to the hospital I was wearing my glasses, which I only wear at home right before bedtime. I desperately wanted my contacts. I wanted to look at myself in the mirror and see me again.

Where had I gone?

CHAPTER 14

The Outside World

I was finally feeling strong enough to talk to my family, but I was scared to let them into my mind, afraid that missing them would be too much for me to handle.

My mom came to visit that day and brought me some of her clothes to wear. I was excited to see her but worried she was going to get too emotional, which would in turn make me more emotional and I was already pretty unsteady.

I wanted people to be completely void of emotion when talking to me. I also didn't want to hear about anything bad or about how my family was doing. I was like a fragile egg that if touched just a little too hard, would crack.

Fortunately, she stayed strong for me. She said that I looked better than what she had expected. She told me later that my hair was brushed and I was wearing makeup. My mom thought I looked fine from the outside, but what was happening inside me was a whole different story.

My mom grew up dealing with mental illness. She visited her father many times in a mental hospital, so to her this wasn't anything new. It was just new now that it was happening to her daughter.

I was amazed at her strength when she visited me in the hospital. I was afraid it would bring back bad memories of her father, but at least on the outside, it didn't.

Back at home, things weren't going so well for my family. My husband's back was still hurting terribly. But instead of being able to rest and heal it, he was now the one up all night with the baby then taking care of all three kids during the day. His mother was there to help, but he had a difficult time surrendering control to anyone else. The kids had already lost a mother; he didn't want them to not have their father around either.

Unlike me, however, he didn't try to be *Superman*—it was more like *Survivor*. He quit taking Evan to school, stopped answering phone calls, and did his best just to get through each day, living with the pain of not knowing when his wife would come home, or if she'd ever be the same again.

He received very little information from the hospital about my condition, yet everyone was hounding him for answers. He couldn't eat and had lost fifteen pounds in a week. He was trying his best to stay strong for the boys and not show an ounce of emotion as many men do.

When I called Eirik on the public phone for the first time, I could tell he was really worn out. I told him not to tell me any details about what was going on at home. I couldn't handle worrying about my family. Just hearing his voice made me feel like my body was an old mirror, and any moment it would shatter into a million pieces.

Eirik felt like he was the cause of my anxiety, and that gave him a lot of guilt. He felt that our home life was to blame for the onset of my illness, and that my talking to him only caused me more distress.

To me it was more the pain of separation that hurt so much, and I knew I needed to minimize that pain as much as possible to get myself better.

At first I could only handle short conversations; I just said a quick "hello" and hung up. It made me too depressed to talk to my family not knowing when I'd see them again. I would choke back the tears, trying not to tailspin back into another panic attack. It was just easier to pretend they didn't exist.

My mother-in-law had gone home for a week, but Eirik had already missed two weeks of work and needed to get back. Sylvia drove back to Minneapolis from Des Moines to stay with my family indefinitely.

I had gotten wind that Sylvia was nervous about taking care of three small children herself. After all, it had been several decades since she'd raised her kids.

This uncertainty made me worry tremendously about my family.

Are they going to make it?

The boys took this time to test Grandma Sylvia's patience. They didn't always listen to Grandma's rules and ran around the house like crazed chickens.

I'm sure that this time was so confusing to the boys. Mom goes to the hospital. Mom brings home a new baby. Then Mom is gone. Where is she? When is she coming home? No one could answer this for them.

To this day they seem to have a separation anxiety from me that wasn't there before. When I went away for a few days on a business trip, they constantly wanted to know when I would return. I can't even go to the bathroom without Eithan screaming in terror.

I heard that my brother and his wife Erin called my parents and husband daily for updates. They had seen how I was acting when they were in town and knew that something really serious was going on.

My brother mentioned many months later that I seemed distant and withdrawn when he had visited. He said I would hold and nurse Emily, but it was like I wasn't really there. I was this empty shadow of a mom, and it pains me hearing that.

My doctor thought I was doing better and gave me a pass to go see the outside world for a few hours. We decided it might not be a good idea to see Eirik and the kids right away, so my dad came to take me out to dinner. Eirik was understanding and just wanted what was best for me.

I nervously paced the hallways all day waiting for the time to come when he would pick me up. I couldn't even remember what outside air felt like anymore. When I saw him coming to the double locked doors, he looked terrified. I could tell he was trying really hard to hold back his emotions for me. When I saw him, we hugged and his voice was all shaky. I have hardly ever seen my dad cry before. The only time I can remember is when my parents got divorced when I was eight years old.

I wanted to go to Target to get a watch. I thought this would help me remember when it was group time. Then we decided to get dinner at Perkins.

I got really dizzy when I looked at anything other than my dad. Bright lights really bothered my eyes. The outside world was just too overwhelming. As long as I looked at his face and nothing else, I felt okay for a few minutes at a time.

The doctor later told me that I was experiencing a condition called sensory overload, which seemed logical. The more stimuli around me, the more confusing everything felt.

Since my first pass went well, my doctor thought it was time to see my husband and the baby. This caused me a great deal of anxiety all day because I wasn't sure how I would react to them. I nervously paced up and down the blue carpeted hallway for hours.

I wish the staff could have offered me more guidance and support to get through this challenging day, but I wasn't given the individual attention that I wanted. Cara was going on a pass with her family that night too and was very scared. We both found comfort in each other's fears.

When Eirik and Emily arrived at the hospital, I took one look at my daughter and felt like I didn't even know her anymore. She had gone from a one-month old to a six-week-old and she had changed so much. Her face was fuller, her hair was lighter, and she was a lot more alert.

I choked up trying to hold back my tears. I missed my family so much. I missed my baby.

Will I ever get to watch her grow?

My husband handled her with ease, delicately taking her in and out of her car seat. I didn't like how he had dressed her. She was wearing white sleepers with purple flowers on it in the evening. I would have never dressed her in pajamas to go out to dinner. I would have put her in a nice dress.

Why is Eirik taking over my job?

I resented him for the bond he had with Emily. I took her out of her carrier and held her, but it seemed like I was holding someone else's baby.

Who is this child? Does she even recognize me? Does she know I am her mother?

I was completely disconnected. I felt like I had missed out on so much. I had been robbed of the newborn stage with my last baby, when I had such carefully laid-out plans of cherishing every precious newborn moment.

We decided to go to a nearby restaurant for dinner. It felt really awkward—kind of like a first date. Neither one of us really knew what to say to each other. Eirik walked on eggshells trying not to say anything to upset me, but he was so stressed out and tired and just wanted someone to talk to.

During dinner he told me how well Emily was doing bottle feeding, what her sleeping schedule was, what he was having her wear, and the cute faces she would make.

I felt like I didn't even know my own daughter and that my place as a mother in my family had been taken away from me.

I am the one who is supposed to be doing those motherly things!

There were a few more things I wanted to pick up from the store, so we stopped by Target on the way back. When we were there, everything started to feel surreal. I nervously paced the aisles, not sure what I was looking for. Everything started speeding up again and spinning. I couldn't find Eirik and Emily.

When I finally found them, I felt really confused.

"Who is that?" I said to Eirik about the baby.

"It's our daughter," he replied.

"What's her name?" I asked.

While at the store, we ran into my friend Cara from the hospital. I was so happy to see a familiar face. It was really strange, but I felt more at home seeing her then I did with my own family. It was as if she was the only other human being in the world who understood what was happening to me on the inside. We were in this strange new world together that outsiders just didn't get.

Eirik decided we needed to leave right away and drove me back to the hospital. We sat in the car on a cold and rainy October evening and I pleaded to him, "Please don't leave me. I don't want you to go. I want to go home. Don't make me stay in that awful place," I cried.

"That's where you need to be right now. You need to get better," he said.

When I got back to the hospital, I sobbed uncontrollably for hours. I couldn't stand the thought of not going home with my family.

Then somehow, I got up the strength to go to wrap-up session, which was an end of the day meeting to talk about your day. I told the other patients how I saw my husband and baby and how sad I was to leave them, but how joyous it felt to be reunited again. I then felt proud of myself for getting through the evening, even if it didn't go as well as I had hoped.

At a recent therapy session that Eirik and I went to to deal with our grief from this experience, Eirik revealed some shocking news to me.

He said that he was terrified of me that night. He felt like he was with a stranger. He didn't know what I was capable of doing to Emily and clung onto her tightly, keeping me always at a safe distance from her. He didn't know what had happened to his wife, or if the real Stacey would ever return. This wasn't the loving, gentle wife he had married.

He felt a tremendous loss and started thinking about how he would raise these kids alone.

My doctor encouraged me to keep trying out the passes and said that a few setbacks just meant I'm not ready to go home yet, and that I need to take smaller steps.

This was a big disappointment because we were discussing my discharge earlier that week, and now freedom seemed so out of reach.

The following night I went to one of my favorite restaurants, the Cheesecake Factory, with my dad. I felt much better this time and was able to carry on a fairly normal conversation as long as I focused intently.

My meal was so large that I brought a bunch of leftovers back to the hospital. It tasted really good after all of the hospital food. Once I was able to eat again, I had been living on chocolate cake. Even though I should have been trying to lose the baby weight, I felt like dessert was one of the few joys that I had left in my life, so I ate it without regret.

The next evening I offered to share my restaurant meal with the other residents. One man, an older gentleman who had just checked in a few days prior, I am pretty certain was homeless. He was someone who had chronic mental health issues and lived in various group home settings. He was so excited to eat my leftovers. I am not sure if he had eaten a restaurant meal in years. I decided not to finish my dinner and give it to him because it really made his day.

While I started to develop more trust with the people around me, I just wanted to be better and get home. I felt that this recovery took too long and I wanted immediate action. I was desperate to try anything.

I got wind that one of the residents was getting electroconvulsive therapy (ECT). I begged my doctor to give me the treatment.

He said, "You are really far from needing ECT. That only comes as a last resort."

I felt like this was the final straw. I needed to heal now. I needed my life back! I couldn't go another hour without being a mother to my children.

That night I wrote the following entry in my journal:

It seems like the floor has collapsed.
Like there is no lower place to fall.
Is this all a bad dream?
I just have to have faith in the power that's above.
I will get better.
I will get better.
I can make it.
I can do it.

CHAPTER 15

The Apple Doesn't Fall Far from the Tree

Monday, November 2, 2009

Going home was scarier than staying. It was like letting a chimpanzee out of the zoo and wishing him a nice life in the wild.

I requested a family meeting to talk about my discharge. I was supposed to be sent home that day, but after the disassociation and breakdown that occurred after my night out with Eirik and Emily, it was postponed.

Just trying to coordinate the family meeting was stressful. My mom was supposed to babysit the kids that day, but she wanted to be at the hospital. I told her that she needed to find someone else to babysit and that I couldn't deal with it. She found a neighbor to take all three kids and was able to come.

The family meeting took place in a conference room between two locked doors of the unit. Dr. Wilson was there, along with a social worker and my mom, dad, and husband.

Eirik looked pale and exhausted and sat quietly during the meeting trying to take everything in.

My parents were extremely anxious, and similarly to me, wanted answers to all of their questions. I can't blame them; if it were my child, I would react the same way.

During the meeting, everyone talked about me like I was a fly on the wall.

"What's happening to my daughter?" my mom pleaded.

She had been calling the hospital daily, but it was still difficult for her to get any real information.

They explained that I had suffered from postpartum anxiety and panic disorder, along with some psychotic episodes. The doctor said that my condition was improving and that the psychotic episodes had resolved. The biggest hurdle I needed to get over was to believe I would get better. The doctor said if I stayed healthy for one year after the breakdown, it was unlikely this would ever happen again. If I continued to have panic attacks, it could be related to our family history of mental illness.

I had written in my journal what I would need from my family once I got home. This was a very difficult thing to do, as I'm normally the caregiver, not the patient.

1. Sleep through the night.
2. At first, being home but not taking any responsibility for the kids or the house.
3. People talking to me one at a time in a very calm tone.
4. No arguing / fighting.
5. Do not talk about stresses, even if they are there.
6. Someone to come into the house who can take full responsibility for the kids.
7. Someone to drive me to therapy.

We talked about my transition out of the hospital. I had requested to the social worker before this meeting that she come up with a plan for me to get help once I got home, but she never met with me. It may have been because her case load was too full, but nonetheless, I felt unheard.

If I could change one thing about the current system, it would be to have better transitional care to home put in place for new moms. Having a home health nurse come to visit would have eased a lot of my anxiety, plus it could have shortened my hospital stay.

I realized that I was on my own here and I was terrified to go home and face the responsibilities of being a mom of three. I suggested staying at my mom's house for a little while where it would be quieter, and I wouldn't have any parenting responsibility. I also thought about staying at my great-aunt Sophie's house. A quiet apartment without any kids sounded like a great idea, but the doctor immediately dismissed it, saying that isolation would not be healthy.

At the end of the meeting, we agreed that I would go to my mom's house for the first week. I felt pretty good about how the meeting had gone and was excited but scared to be discharged.

Later that day, Dr. Wilson stopped me in the hallway and said, "You're not going to your mom's house."

"What do you mean?" I asked.

I thought we had come up with a good plan.

"The apple doesn't fall far from the tree," he said. "Your mother is more anxious than you are!"

I always knew that my parents were worriers. They wear their emotions on their sleeves, unlike my husband's family that tends to keep their feelings very private.

That day, a discharge plan was made for me to continue on my current medications until I could find a psychiatrist outside of the hospital, meet with a counselor for one-on-one sessions once a week, and attend a four-week intensive outpatient program that focuses on behavioral therapy.

There still wasn't a plan in place for how to handle things at home or to get help caring for my kids, which made me very anxious. I wasn't feeling comfortable at all being left alone with my children.

What if I have another panic attack? What if I become psychotic again and put my kids in harm's way? I just can't live with myself if that happened. Why are they sending me back into the fire? I can't even take care of myself! It seems irresponsible to leave three little lives in my care.

After the meeting, the staff wrote up the following discharge notes that summarized my hospitalization and analyzed my behavior at this time:

> Ms. Ackerman was alert, oriented, and cooperative. Answered questions appropriately. Speech was regular rate and rhythm, normal volume and tone. Thought process was goal intact. Thought content was negative for suicidal ideation, negative for plan or intent. Negative for obsessions, compulsions or psychosis. Her mood was much improved, but still anxious. Her affect was dramatically improved. She was much more capable of interacting with people. She did have some lability. Her insight was improving. She still quite easily, though, could upset herself by misinterpreting physical symptoms.

CHAPTER 16

New Residents

Am I the most mentally-ill person ever to come to the psych ward? Am I going to be written about in Guinness Book of World Records as the incurable postpartum anxiety patient? I desperately want to go home before everyone forgets about my existence.

By now, the second group of residents including my friend Cara had already left. I couldn't believe I would remain here.

That afternoon, a volunteer came to the occupational therapy room and played his guitar and sang songs about his experience with bipolar disorder. He had written the music in the midst of a manic episode.

I closed my eyes and truly relaxed for the first time in weeks. I just let the music move me. His music calmed me, and it was a nice peaceful escape. It gave me a sense of hope just meeting someone else that had suffered and was healed.

When I first went to the occupational therapy sessions, I could barely hold a paintbrush. My hand would tremble and shake, and if I tried to do anything it looked worse than a painting my two-year-old could make.

Now I decided I felt well enough to make something for my kids. I felt great joy in being able to give them a present—a so-called souvenir of my *vacation*.

While I was still much slower than normal and concentrating was difficult, I tried my best to paint a wooden puzzle for each of my kids. I wrote Emily's name on one of them and painted it bright pink to match her room. It sits on her bookshelf today and is a constant reminder of how grateful I am for her.

I was finally at the point of feeling like I wanted to reach out to people beyond my family. There was a slow, old desktop computer that was open for an hour a day. It was shared between all of the residents. Patients could use the Internet during occupational therapy, but there was a bitter, hard-of-hearing old lady looking over your shoulder, reading every word you wrote to make sure that you weren't sending out any *insane* messages.

I decided to type an e-mail to all of my friends and extended family members letting them know what happened. I asked them to make sure that Eirik and the kids were okay. Eirik was upset that I had done this because he didn't want help from anybody. He just wanted to be left alone.

From this came a generous outreach of support. In fact Eirik received so many phone calls he couldn't keep up with them all, which actually ended up causing him more stress because he likes to handle problems alone.

However, this outreach made me realize what a great support system our family has. So many of the residents were all alone and had no one to come home to, while I had so many wonderful people in my life who cared.

I did, however, have some negative reactions to this public outreach by certain family members. They thought that this matter should be kept private, and that it could be harmful to my career and reputation. I didn't care though; I just wanted to make sure that Eirik could get the support he needed.

In recent days he confessed to me that there were times when I was in the hospital that he was jealous and wished we could trade places. While everyone saw me as the patient and I got help, he was suffering in silence. As an introvert and a do-it-yourselfer, he didn't want to talk to anyone or ask for help.

Eirik still suffers from some depression and stress-related heart problems, which he recently got on medication for. I wish that I had been aware of some type of therapy or support group that my husband and parents could have attended. While I was the patient, I believe that a crisis like this is extremely difficult for family members as well.

While in occupational therapy one day, I started talking to a woman in her fifties named Linda. Every day at group check in and check out she recited the same prayer. Every day she paced up and down the halls quietly mumbling. I had never really heard her speak before. She told me that day that she had a PhD and was a professor. When she started talking, I could tell she was extremely intelligent.

How does someone like that get to this place?

It is interesting that some of the smartest people out there can become victims of mental illness. It reminded me of the movie *A Beautiful Mind*, where a highly respectable professor lost his mind.

I really never learned Linda's story; she wasn't very open to sharing it with anyone. All I know is that she had been in the hospital for a long, long time (even longer than me). She often stayed in her room and didn't like to participate with others. She seemed to have a social phobia. Linda also had a court case she kept mentioning, but I never learned the details. I was really drawn to her because she seemed so quiet and mysterious, but I knew there was a lot more to her than the eye could see.

As old patients moved out, new ones moved in. Unfortunately, these new patients were a little bit different from the first two groups of people I met.

I finally slept through the night thanks to mass doses of sleeping pills. However, one night, I was awakened hearing screaming outside of my door. We weren't allowed to close our doors for security purposes, so every noise came right into the room.

This woman verbally abused the staff and every other word was, "Fuck this and fuck that!" I was pretty frightened by her outlandish behavior. She told us at group that her name was Kaneesha and that she was in a gang. She was pregnant and her other children had been taken away from her. She was also a heavy drug user and seller.

Later that day, a fight broke out between Kaneesha and some of the other residents. I'm not sure what the fight was all about. Being a middle-class suburban mom, I had never seen gang fighting before. I hid in my room, terrified to come out. I was paranoid of people because of my illness, but even the *real* Stacey would have been scared in this situation.

Kaneesha was sent to solitary confinement until someone could pick her up. The hospital kicked her out and said they couldn't help someone like her. Her mother came and got her and said that she gets into trouble like this all of the time, and that she's beyond the point of being able to get help. I felt sad for her—her own mother had given up on her.

How does someone get to that point in their life?

Another equally interesting patient had checked into the ward. I can't remember her name, but I'll call her Mrs. D. for diamond. Apparently she had on a ten-carat diamond, but the hospital had confiscated it for security purposes.

Mrs. D. looked like she would be really pretty if she was cleaned up. She was in her thirties, had beautiful blond, hair and was model thin but constantly stuffed her face and left mounds of garbage everywhere. She was also a yeller. She yelled and yelled and yelled about how she wanted out of this fucking place!

She was a multimillionaire who had lost it all. Her husband had just gotten out of jail for drugs and she was about to see him for the first time in two years, but she was ordered to the behavioral health unit.

Mrs. D. wanted to get help for her alcoholism. She claimed she was going to kill herself, but she later confessed that it was a scam to get her insurance company to cover her visit. Her insurance carrier would cover a mental health stay for suicide but not for drug and alcohol addiction. Because of her suicidal status, she was put on a twenty-four-hour hold in the unit. Now she was regretting her decision to lie and wanted to leave.

It is really sad that people in this country have to go to such extremes to get proper care.

Another newcomer was Sharon. She had piercing blue eyes and looked evil. Sharon would never make eye contact with anyone.

I wished the hospital could give us a psychological profile of everyone we encountered so we could better understand how to communicate with them. "She has social phobia, don't go near her." Or, "He thinks that everyone is the devil, so stay away." This kind of information would have been very useful but an obvious breach of confidentiality.

Anyway, Sharon had pointy teeth too that made her seem even more devilish. She was in her late twenties or early thirties and would never talk. She just stared into space. Everyone was afraid of her. Later on during my stay, I saw that she had empathy. When I talked about my children she looked at me with concern, but Sharon still didn't speak. I am sure that something was terribly wrong with her; I just never learned what it was.

I also met Jan, who had a strong impact on me. She was a woman about my age with medium-length mousy blond hair. Jan was a frequent flyer of the psychiatric ward. She kept telling me how this hospital is evil and how the doctors are going to poison my mind. She said we are treated like prisoners, without any respect. She said that I should request a hospital transfer because this place would never help me get well.

She really scared me and made me feel hopeless. I decided to avoid Jan from then on, realizing that I had already made the choice to be in this hospital and that I wanted to make the most of the situation, not live in even more fear.

I started feeling claustrophobic at the hospital and wanted to get some exercise. There wasn't much room, so I started walking briskly up and down the halls.

I found an old exercise bike. I was always the first one up in the morning, so I started getting on this clunky old bike.

One day I discovered that the ward had a Pilates VHS tape. While the tape was really dated, I decided that the workout would be worth doing. It was locked and I had to get an assistant to get it for me, but I discovered they also had Pilates mats and exercise bands.

I was so excited by the ability to do something that I would in my normal life, and I quickly told the other residents about it. Before I knew it, I had started a Pilates class with four other female residents, and a few more just watched. I was definitely getting a piece of the old Stacey back.

I found that the exercise helped clear my mind and helped me and the other residents feel a sense of normalcy. It also helped us to pass the time during these long days.

I truly believe that all patients suffering from mental health disorders should be encouraged to be physically active if they are able to, and I wish the hospital had made it more accessible.

Every morning I would meet with Dr. Wilson in a conference room with a window behind two double-locked doors. There was a large window overlooking the city, a round table, and two chairs.

I obsessively waited each day for Dr. Wilson to see me for these daily meetings. I wanted to be the first person he saw each morning. I would pace back and forth at the nurses' station, watching the doctor through the glass windows.

I wanted my questions answered—*now*. I had this strange narcissism at the time which made me think that I was suffering more than anyone else, and therefore I deserved the most attention from the doctor.

I wanted answers and I wanted hope. I felt like he was the only one who could do that. He had the ultimate power. While his abrasiveness often turned me and the other patients off, I believed that he knew what he was talking about and had knowledge that the nurses and social workers didn't have.

I decided to start writing down my moods, along with questions for the doctor. I thought this would make our meetings more efficient, which they did.

Here are some excerpts from my notes:

Day 1
Groggy, spaced out, nervous, scared of new people, worried I won't ever get better, bored, hopeless, desperate

Day 2
Woke up feeling good; not groggy, clear head, but anxious and a bit trembly; memory good; good the rest of the day

Day 3
6 AM – Felt good but jittery
8 AM – Nervous, jittery, clear head

CHAPTER 17

The Ultimate Panic Attack

Tuesday, November 3, 2009

I woke up having a panic attack that felt like a deadly earthquake. I couldn't breathe, I couldn't concentrate, and I was fearful of everything.

I sprung out of bed from a nightmare about going home. I pictured my children suffering because I couldn't take care of them. Suddenly, I didn't want to go home. It seemed like an even scarier place than the hospital, if that was possible!

Until this point, I slept in a medical bed that was closer to the nurses' station because of my fall on the first day. That morning there was a patient in the hospital that needed the medical bed I was sleeping on, and I was told I'd have to move down the hall.

The normal Stacey is pretty go-with-the-flow and wouldn't have really cared, but this new Stacey didn't like the idea at all! I was terrified of having a different roommate. I had really learned to trust and confide in Cherise, and I wasn't in the mood to make another friend.

The psych assistant Dave yelled at me several times to move my stuff. There were some really great assistants in the hospital, and then there were ones like Dave who liked to treat patients like helpless children.

I ignored him. I didn't want to move. I was terrified of a new environment, even if it was only down the hall. He didn't show a lot of compassion for my ultraparanoid state. Each new environment I faced became a very scary place. I procrastinated moving my stuff as long as I could until I practically got dragged down there by Dave, who I thought would throw my belongings down the hall if I didn't hurry along.

When I got to the room and saw the bed, I was horrified! It was in the middle of the room; it was about as wide as I am and was a thin mattress on top of a solid wood frame that couldn't be moved.

I found Dave and yelled to him, "There is no way I'm sleeping in that bed!" I showed him my wristband and said, "Look, I'm a fall risk. I'm going to fall out of that bed. It's not safe."

The guy was a real jerk and told me I would sleep there and that's that.

Screw you! Try and make me sleep there!

I took my mattress and set it on the floor.

That's where I'll sleep and they can't make me move!

Luckily, no one said anything that night about my insistence of sleeping on the floor.

My new roommate was a teenage girl from the same town as me. She was on drugs and had tried to commit suicide. I wasn't sure what to think of her, and I wasn't really in the mood to get to know her. She didn't do much talking to me either. We just kept to ourselves inside the tiny hospital room.

Several times that day I tried to read a book or write in my journal on my new floor bed. The words in the book were there, but I couldn't get them to make sense in my brain. They were just words on a page. They danced around like little elves but wouldn't come inside my mind. At home, reading in bed always relaxes me, but it just wouldn't work and I grew increasingly frustrated.

I also tried writing in my journal, another source of clearing my head in my *real* life. When I write, I get lost in the words and forget about the world happening around me. But I couldn't write either. The pen just shook in my hand and my brain was void of any thoughts that I could transcribe to paper, yet the messages in my mind were racing by like runners in a marathon.

I nervously paced the halls all day. I couldn't stop feeling like I would die. My heart raced. I trembled all over.

Why is this happening now?

I was certain they were never going to send me home.

Maybe that's a good thing. Then my children will be safe.

There was a priest who frequently visited the hospital. I am not a Christian, but I latched onto him. Maybe he could give me hope. We were in the middle of the hallway and I said to him, "Hold me. Please hold me. I'm scared."

At first he gave me a confused look, but then I grabbed his hand. When I touched him, I realized how painful the separation from my baby was.

After just giving birth, I felt this terrible emptiness inside by not being near her. I just wanted to touch someone, to feel human again. To know that there was hope. Somehow, human touch grounded me. It made me feel real.

His touch helped connect me, but the panic attack still didn't stop. One of the assistants offered to play a game with me and I chose Yahtzee, a game I loved playing both as a child and as an adult with my husband. I was still nervous as hell, but it helped me to get my mind off things for a little while.

The trouble I had with the game, however, is that I couldn't add the numbers together very well. I was much slower than normal at even the simplest things. I wondered how I would ever function again in society.

Will I be able to ever get another professional job?

Later that night the assistant asked me if I wanted to go for a walk into the main part of the hospital. I thought that would be a good idea. We walked all around. I was still feeling pretty dizzy, so I'd stop and sit on a bench every few minutes. It was weird to see the regular hospital. It reminded me of just a few weeks earlier when I had given birth, and what a happy time in my life that was. It felt like a lifetime ago.

Was that my life, or was it someone else's?

We finally made it back to a lounge area right outside of the locked unit. I asked to sit down. I took a few deep breaths and suddenly the panic attack stopped. It had lasted for ten straight hours. It was definitely a supersized panic attack as far as panic attacks go. But I got through it. I was going to be okay.

CHAPTER 18

Going Home

Wednesday, November 4, 2009

"I don't think there's anything we can do for you here anymore," the doctor said.

He told me to go home for a few hours that night for a trial reunion and then do the real thing the next day.

"Seriously!" I shouted. "You heard what happened to me yesterday. What if that happens at home?"

"It probably will," he said. "But there's nothing more we can do for you here. We've gotten in a lot of new patients, and some of them are doing you more harm than good," he said.

I called my husband to tell him the good news, but his reaction wasn't at all what I'd hoped for.

"I can't take care of you too," he said. "I'm so stressed out taking care of three kids, going to work, not sleeping. I'm worried that you're going to be more work for me."

Wow, this really made me feel like crap. I thought he would be overjoyed to have his wife back. His reaction wasn't at all what I expected, but knowing now the hell he was going through, I can see why he said this. I told him I would try not to ask him for any help, and my dad said he could come over if I needed him.

At the same time Cherise, who was the only one who had been hospitalized longer than I had, would move to a halfway house. She was going to live in a group home for people who are highly suicidal. She left before me and we didn't get a chance to say goodbye. The hall phone rang for me later that day and it was Cherise wishing me well. I prayed for her safety.

Later that afternoon, Eirik was going to pick me up from the hospital and take me home for just a few hours. I was really anxious all day.

How will I be around the kids? Can I hold myself together for them?

I hadn't seen my boys in almost two weeks—I had never left them for so long. And when I'd seen my baby last time, my reaction was not good. I sat in the hallway all day just looking at the Exit sign on the door and wondering what life outside would be like. I tried for hours to read the same magazine article, but the pages just stared back at me.

The drive from the hospital to home was a nerve-wracking one for both of us. After the incident at Target, Eirik wasn't quite sure what I was capable of doing and it terrified him. He was afraid to tell me anything about what was going on at home for fear I would break down.

He turned on the radio and we drove in silence for what seemed like an eternity. Then the song "You May Be Right" by Billy Joel came on the air. I thought this was really funny and I started bolting out the lyrics, "You may be right; I may be crazy; but it just might be a lunatic you're looking for ..."

I don't think Eirik found this to be quite as funny as I did at the time because he was under so much stress, but normally this would have been just his type of humor. It was one of the only times during this ordeal where I was able to find humor in the situation.

As we pulled into the garage, I was terrified to walk in. My heart started pounding. I tried some of the breathing techniques, one of the few useful things that I learned in group therapy. I stood up tall, locked my arms down straight, clenched my fists, and squeezed as hard as I could in this position until I could physically feel the tension going out of my body. I was afraid of what life at home would be like. I wanted to go back to the hospital where I knew I would be safe.

My two boys ran to the door as we pulled in and greeted me with big bear hugs. It felt like a lifetime since I'd seen them. I was afraid they had forgotten me, but they seemed to remember me just fine.

I choked away tears because I wanted to stay strong for my boys and not have them see me as an emotional train wreck. I was terrified to be their mother again and didn't feel at all capable to do so.

Regardless, I was so happy to be able to be back in their lives, even if it was just as an observer. For a while, I thought this reunion would never come.

My mother-in-law, Sylvia, was holding baby Emily. She planned to stay with me and the kids until I could handle them on my own, but I could tell she was anxious to get back to her own life in Iowa. She had been in town when I was hospitalized, went home for a little while, and had returned back to Minnesota so Eirik could go back to work.

I just looked at Emily, afraid to pick her up for fear I would drop her, or worse, that she wouldn't remember me.

Sylvia told me that she would take charge of the baby, but whenever I wanted to step in I just had to ask. I told her that I wanted to hold Emily. I held her in my arms, but she was a stranger to me. I quickly gave her back like she was a hot potato.

I felt like I visited someone else's house. It was horribly painful to watch my mother-in-law handle my baby so effortlessly. I was glad they had bonded but also jealous that my bond with Emily seemed to be missing.

When I got home, I looked around feeling like I was in a strange place, yet so many things were exactly like I left them. The wood floors seemed to be much brighter and shinier, but I think my medication distorted my eyesight, making me see things much more vibrantly. Eirik assured me that he had no time to wax the floors while I was gone!

Before I was admitted to the hospital, I had left several things out of place, another thing that caused me a lot of anxiety. There was a bin of old kids' clothes sitting out that I had gone through when my brother was in town. It sat exactly where I had left it. The Halloween cookies that we made that gave me the strange hallucinations were still in the cookie jar. It was as if time had stood still, yet I had missed so much.

I was definitely walking on eggshells that night. I was trying so hard to appear *normal*. Sylvia cooked dinner and I was actually able to sit down and eat a meal with my family this time. She said I seemed a lot better than when I had left.

Having to leave my kids again that night to go back to the hospital was extremely painful. I didn't want to ever have to leave them again.

What if Dr. Wilson decides not to let me out again?

When I returned to the hospital, I was sent back to my old room but with a new roommate, the woman who needed the hospital bed. Her name was Charlotte and she was very Southern. She was a short, round woman with pale skin, bright blue eyes, and dark brown hair. She walked with canes because she had a debilitating disease. Charlotte was only about forty, but she seemed much older. She had tried to commit suicide because she didn't like living with her disease.

This time around, I was okay with the roommate change. Maybe because I knew I was going home soon.

Thursday, November 5, 2009

The next morning Charlotte yelled, "Help me! Please get a nurse."

I ran down the hall and into our room to see what was going on. She had leaked diarrhea all through the hallway and needed help getting new clothes. I was disgusted—I can barely stand cleaning up diarrhea from my own kids, and looking at the mess from a grown woman was awful.

I ran up to the nurses' station and an assistant came to help Charlotte get cleaned up. The smell was overwhelming and it carried through the entire enclosed unit, which of course didn't have any windows that opened. I thought I was going to throw up from the fumes.

Just then a phone call came in for me and I answered it. Right after that I realized it was the phone that Charlotte was just on, which hadn't been disinfected. I then looked down and noticed I was standing in her poop—the staff hadn't had time to clean it up yet.

That day my dad was picking me up for my permanent return home. I had to see the doctor and get some paper work taken care of before they would release me, and I was told it would take until about 2:00 pm. Eirik would still be at work, and I'd have a few hours with the kids and Grandma Sylvia before he returned.

I was so scared that I would forget to take my medications at home. After all, inside the hospital, I always had someone to remind me. I was also terrified that I would have a breakdown in front of my kids. Worst of all, I feared that I wouldn't be able to make it at home, and I'd wind up right back in the mental institution.

I planned to go around and say goodbye to everyone, but as soon as my dad arrived I said, "Let's get the hell out of here!" and I fled as fast as I could without ever turning back.

On the drive home I used the deep breathing techniques that I learned in the hospital. I was overwhelmed by the sun, the cars, the buildings, and the bright big world in front of me. The combination of medications and sensory overload I experienced made everything I saw or heard extremely magnified. I had gotten used to living such a confined life that the outside world seemed like a big scary place.

When I entered my home, I was greeted by two very excited boys. "Mommy!" they exclaimed. Just a few short weeks earlier I didn't think this reunion would ever be possible. I was so excited to see them, but I held back my tears of joy to keep my emotions in check.

Grandma Sylvia was holding the baby again. I was still terrified to touch her. I thought I would drop her. I felt completely incompetent of taking care of her. Sylvia assured me she would take over watching the kids and the household, but I could jump in any time that I felt ready. I wasn't sure that time would ever come.

What will I do when she leaves?

I watched her hold and feed the baby. I felt completely disconnected to her.

Is this really my child?

Everything over the past six weeks just felt like a really bad dream. Sylvia told me all about her routine, how she likes her bottle, when she gets up, what her different cries mean.

Is this her baby?

Don't get me wrong; I was grateful for the help and I couldn't have done it without her, but I felt like I'd been replaced.

Eirik returned from work a few hours later and we were finally all reunited as a family. It still wasn't normal though, and I felt like I was watching someone else's family from a window.

At night, I was terrified of the dark. I asked Eirik to keep the bathroom light on, the hall light on, and the door open. I had developed this crazy startle reflex in the hospital, and every little noise made me jump and gasp; I felt like I was crawling out of my own skin.

Lying in bed that first night, I still felt like I was in the hospital. Then I would open my eyes and see my home. I felt really confused.

What is my life?

I had grown so accustomed to the hospital that my home now felt like the terrifying place.

Will I ever be back to normal?

CHAPTER 19

Visit from Child Protection

I didn't know how I was going to take care of my kids and this caused a lot of anxiety for someone who was trying to recover from anxiety!

I really wished the social workers at the hospital would have helped me come up with a transition plan, but they left me to figure it out on my own.

What I was really hoping for was someone to be able to stay with me and the kids while Eirik went to work just to make sure that we were safe. I was still afraid of my own actions. I didn't have any thoughts of killing my children, but I also didn't trust my mind for things like giving Eithan his medication, or just being physically able to meet the demands of three young kids.

I felt let down by the lack of transitional care provided. It didn't seem right to bring me from incarceration to full responsibility for child care right away.

My dad in his desperation to find me some help, called the county to see if I was eligible for any home health benefits. He was also disappointed in *the system* and felt we were left in a lurch.

My husband had already taken a ton of time off of work—two weeks for paternity leave, another week when I got sick, and the first week I was in the hospital. He was worried he would lose his job if he stayed home any longer.

My parents had also taken several days off of work to help us out during this crisis. My family was running out of time to be able help me if they wanted to keep their jobs.

The county sent out a child protection agent to our house. I was livid! I loved my children very much and was concerned about their safety. I wanted someone to help me, not interrogate me.

The child protection agent visited just a few days after I returned home. She was there for more than two hours. I was still having a difficult time concentrating and holding a conversation with anyone, so the visit was extremely stressful.

While she was talking to me, I worried about my kids. Grandma Sylvia was still there, but she was exhausted and having a difficult time taking care of them all on her own.

The social worker asked me a million questions. "Are you on drugs?" "Do you drink?" "Were you ever abused?"

I understood that this was her job, but why couldn't anyone get me the kind of help I needed, not add more stress to my life!

The child protection agent finally left. She said she was going on vacation for a week, but when she got back she would see if the county would pay for me to send my children to day care for a few weeks.

The problem was I didn't want them to go to day care. I missed them terribly and wanted to be around them. I just wanted someone to be home with me in case I had a panic attack. I didn't want to leave my children wondering what was happening to their mother. I felt very frustrated by this situation.

When I quit my job, I had planned to pick up some kind of part-time work. Now I didn't know when I'd ever have the mental ability to be able to work again—if ever. I started worrying a lot about our finances.

The hospital stay was $1,000 a day and I didn't know how much of that would be covered by insurance. I had taken out a hospitalization insurance policy and hoped that I could get paid from it to relieve some of the financial stress we were facing. When I checked the fine print of the policy it stated, "Excludes hospitalization for mental health."

I couldn't believe it! My hospitalization was for an illness, and a very serious one at that! I was so upset that our country doesn't view mental health the same way it would cancer, a heart attack, or any other physical illness.

The child protection agent tried tracking down Eirik like a hawk, but they played phone tag. Eirik was so busy at work trying to get caught up from all of his missed time that he didn't really have time to deal with the pesky social worker.

She said she needed a meeting with Eirik and wanted to question my neighbors about my mental state. I am not sure why—I think this was just protocol. I suppose they needed to know if what I was saying was true. Once again, I felt like a criminal.

I finally called her back and told her thanks, but I don't need the agency's help anymore and that I'd be just fine with support from family and friends. She really had become more of a burden than someone who could help our family.

I was mailed an action plan that stated things like, "Eirik needs to call home every day to check in on Stacey." This felt really degrading—I didn't feel my husband needed to be my babysitter, and he didn't like the idea of playing that role either.

The agency still hadn't done what we needed—that was to get someone into our home for safety and to relieve some of my anxiety about taking care of the kids. I filled out the form and signed it, but Eirik refused. They finally closed our case.

The hospital's discharge plan was for me to attend a four-week outpatient program. The program ran Monday through Thursday from 9:00 am to 12:30 pm. for four weeks. It was a group setting at an outpatient mental health clinic. Sylvia was leaving in a few days, and I needed to find child care.

I got out a calendar and called family and friends and made a schedule. I had someone scheduled every day for help. This was such a relief. I am so thankful for the many friends and family members that came through to me during such a difficult time.

CHAPTER 20

First Week Home

My first week home went much better than anyone expected, especially me. After that whopper of a panic attack just days earlier in the hospital, I was certain it would happen again, but it didn't.

I continued to be an observer in my home. I watched my mother-in-law take care of the kids and the household, while I tried to stay sane.

After a few days, I wanted to try holding my baby. It felt sad to me that I couldn't nurse her anymore, but I gave her a bottle from me for the first time and she gulped it happily. I guess babies don't really care what kind of milk they get.

For the next week we just stayed home. My son didn't go to school and any activities that were previously on our calendar were cancelled. I didn't talk to anyone but my immediate family. We were just in survival mode. It was like walking on thin ice, just hoping it didn't break.

We were supposed to have a Jewish baby-naming ceremony for Emily in a few weeks, and I had sent out about fifty invitations with her birth announcement.

My mom called everyone to cancel the big event, and suddenly news of my hospitalization became very widespread. I was embarrassed and ashamed by my condition and felt like I was a failure of a mother.

I was really disappointed about cancelling this happy occasion. It was something I had looked forward to for months, but I knew that all of the people and excitement would be too much for me to handle in my fragile state.

After news of my hospitalization became widespread, nothing really changed. I didn't receive any phone calls from relatives to ask how I was doing.

My mom's side of the family has a strong history of mental illness, and it seems like no one wants to acknowledge that it's there. With my illness as well, no one said a word. I also didn't receive any visitors to meet the new baby. I think everyone was afraid to see me.

My husband had the household running so efficiently that I didn't feel like my existence even mattered anymore. When I tried to step in and help with the kids, he told me that wasn't the way they did things anymore and that I was messing up his routine.

I might as well go back to the hospital. No one needs me anymore.

Eirik was just trying to follow my instructions and doing whatever he could to help me hold it together, but I wanted to feel like my family needed me again.

As a mother, I think there is this natural instinct to be in charge of the home and the kids, even in today's modern society of career-minded moms.

While my husband and I normally have a pretty even distribution of labor—he has always been a very hands-on dad—it felt more like he was the one-hundred-percent parent and I was a guest in the home. I just wanted to return to our normal life again.

After a week, my mother-in-law went home. I was really nervous about her departure, but it turned out to be a good thing. It forced me to find my place back in the home.

I started feeding the baby, changing diapers, and hanging out with my kids. My first week without full-time help went much better than expected.

While I was still really sick, I was capable of doing much more than I gave myself credit for. I didn't have any mental breakdowns. I correctly took my medication and gave Eithan the proper dosages of his meds as well.

We still stayed homebound. My goal at this time was just to care for my kids and get through the day until Eirik returned home from work at around 4:30 pm. Just showering, getting dressed, and getting my kids dressed took a major effort. I didn't really interact or play with them much. I constantly feared another breakdown.

I don't know how we survived those first few weeks, but we did and things slowly got better.

Chapter 21

Therapy

After a week back home without ever leaving the house, it was time to face the world again. I started the outpatient program, an intensive behavioral therapy class that Dr. Wilson recommended. This caused me more anxiety because of the juggling of helpers I had to deal with to take care of the kids.

I wished the hospital social worker could have provided me with child-care resources to attend this therapy. I was ashamed and embarrassed to rely on my family and friends once again. I felt like a complete failure that I had to count on other people to take care of my children.

This is my job, and I am failing miserably. Other mothers handle this job so effortlessly, why can't I?

When I first arrived at group, I saw a few familiar faces from the hospital. The first one was Joe, the suburban dad who told me I wasn't crazy. The second one was roommate number two, Celeste, the suicidal teen. It was a weird déjà vu.

The group was led by Dr. Chavel, a psychologist. I explained to him that I was on several high doses of medications and that I could barely stay awake. I also had difficulty concentrating, so I didn't know how much I'd get out of this. He told me that I could stand during the meeting if it helped.

While everyone else sat and listened to his lecture, I paced back and forth in the room, trying my best to concentrate, but it was extremely difficult.

The medication Seroquel had a sedating effect. It is commonly used to treat bipolar disorder and schizophrenia, but it was prescribed for me as an antidepressant. Because of the high level of drugs in my system, I felt like I would pass out at any moment. I don't even know how I drove myself to the meeting because I was a complete zombie.

I tried my best to listen to what Dr. Chavel had to say. He gave a very educational lecture about different types of mental illnesses, but nothing really resonated with my condition. The lectures were very scripted and preassigned and he didn't seem to solicit any feedback from patients. It felt a lot like the college lectures I used to attend at the University of Minnesota, where three hundred students sat in an auditorium as the professor droned on and on.

After group, Joe asked me if I wanted to have lunch with him. He seemed like a nice enough man, so I agreed to do so.

It was so strange eating lunch with him in an actual restaurant, not a hospital. Joe is married and has two young children. His wife had suffered from postpartum depression, so he was very sympathetic to my condition. Joe suffered from bipolar disorder, a condition that causes extreme mood swings—from elation to depression—which resulted in him losing his job.

I continued to go to group for the rest of the week, but I really felt that it wasn't the right place for me. There weren't any other patients attending who were suffering from postpartum mood disorders, and I didn't feel like the lectures were very beneficial.

I told this to Joe and he said, "Maybe it's the place you most need to be right now."

While his words were kind and stuck with me, I decided to search for other available resources that might be a better fit. Most of the people were chronically ill, which only further exasperated my state of doom. While everyone I met was very nice, I was hearing about years of unemployment, poverty, and hopelessness. This only made my situation feel graver.

Is this what my life has become?

I found a women's support group at the same clinic that met one evening a week. I thought this would be a better fit and it would allow me to be home with my kids during the day, decreasing the guilt about leaving them with babysitters and relying on so much help.

When I made the decision to drop out of the day program, I felt a huge sense of relief but hoped I made the right choice. I definitely didn't want to take a step backward. It still didn't make sense to me that I didn't have a social worker to oversee my progress.

The first night I attended the evening program, I met a woman named Jessica who was really frantic.

"Have you been here before?" she asked me.

"No, it's my first night," I said.

"I'm really nervous," she said.

And she was. She was jittery and shaking. It made me anxious just looking at her.

I wondered if that's how I appeared to other people.

Are people seeing something in me that I can't see in myself?

The group leader had a baby too and could relate to my motherly feelings. They were a great group of women, but none of them were there for postpartum mood disorders, and I still felt like the Lone Ranger.

Most of the women in the group were much older than me. I felt like a rookie. These women were chronically ill and had been dealing with their problems for many years.

I wondered if that was what my future had in store for me. I felt the need to flee the meeting. I didn't want to think of myself as *mentally ill*. I just wanted to get back to my normal life.

Most of the women in group were unable to work because their mental illnesses were so severe and debilitating. I loved my career and desperately wanted that piece of me back. I wanted to be more than just a mom, but right then I couldn't even master that task. I didn't know if I'd ever be able to have enough memory and concentration to be able to work at anything other than a minimum-wage job.

I considered applying for disability benefits too, but quickly decided that I wanted to keep fighting to get myself back and not give up.

These other women really scared me. I saw their lives ruined by their illness. They were sad. Some were suicidal. Most were living in poverty.

Please God, don't make this my new life. I want to have my old life back. Will that day ever come?

Karen, a middle-aged woman with dark brown hair and bright red reading glasses told our group how she was alone in her apartment last night and had attempted suicide. This really frightened me.

Will that be me in a few years, so desperate that I feel there is no way out?

These depression groups made me feel depressed.

During that same time period, I was attending one-on-one counseling that the hospital sent me to. These sessions were nice because I had someone to talk to other than my family members who were already emotionally drained from the ordeal.

My counselor, Dori, helped me to prioritize my life so I wouldn't feel overwhelmed. We talked about how to break up my day so I would have a certain amount of time to play with my kids, dedicated time for cleaning, and other ways to organize my schedule. She encouraged me to take on fewer activities and minimize stressors.

While I agree that this was important at the time, I felt completely void of myself. I am a person who thrives on change, new ideas, social activity, and excitement. My life being transformed to taking care of kids, cleaning, and isolation made me feel very down and depressed. I wanted to lead a more fulfilling life than this, but I accepted it for what it was at the time.

At least I am finally home.

At this time I panicked about money. I was still worried I would never be able to return to work again and wondered how my husband would support me and three kids. I didn't qualify from any type of disability insurance, so I felt really torn between a rock and a hard place.

Dori encouraged me not to worry about working yet, but I felt the financial burden that Eirik was under and felt guilty for not being able to help.

My husband and I discussed the situation and it came down to a minimum that I would need to make for us to be able to meet all of our monthly expenses.

My dad didn't want me to stress myself out about finding a part-time job and gave me some money to get through the rough patch. Eirik absolutely hates taking handouts from other people, but he knew we needed the help and didn't decline the offer.

During my recovery I decided that taking care of me was a priority, and I regularly started attending yoga classes at the gym.

The first time I visited the gym, the sensory overload kicked in. I felt dizzy. The room felt surreal. I went through the yoga moves but felt confused about where I was and what I was doing.

Am I still at the hospital? Am I home? Am I dead?

After class I went to sit in the hot tub. I was so dizzy when I walked that I could barely stand. I sat down with a group of older ladies who had just finished a water aerobics class. I felt confused. When I tried to get out of the hot tub, I nearly fell over. One of the women helped me get on my feet again.

When I drove home that night, the street lights were overpowering and bothered my eyes. Luckily, the gym was close by but driving was scary and dangerous.

For the next few weeks, I still drove but only when necessary and rarely at night. In retrospect, this was a very irresponsible thing to do, but driving was my only sense of freedom.

I finally got in to see my eye doctor and learned that my eyesight had drastically worsened after the birth of my daughter, which is a common occurrence after child birth. He gave me a new prescription for my contacts, which also helped with glaring light, and I began to feel much more comfortable driving again.

As the weeks went by, I became more and more confident around my kids. I was still afraid of the dark and had trouble sleeping at night, but I never took any of the sleeping pills that I was sent home with. The sleeping pills had a horrible hangover effect, and dealing with that and three kids seemed worse to me than a little insomnia. I was happy that I never really needed those pills.

Once I was able to fall asleep at night, I slept pretty well. Eirik had taken over the middle-of-the-night feedings, so that helped me tremendously.

I still felt distanced from my baby, but it was getting better with each passing day. My biggest worry at this time was being able to take care of three kids. I thought having Emily was a big mistake and I resented it. Having three kids in four years seemed like a really bad decision. I remember sitting on the couch just staring at my three kids and feeling completely overwhelmed by the responsibility. I would repetitively count them, "one, two, three." Then I just stared at them in disbelief.

How can I be responsible for their lives when I can't even take care of myself? What was I thinking letting Eirik talk me into having another baby? My life and my other children's lives are ruined.

While I was getting better every day, I still had a long way to go. I wasn't sure that the counseling and women's group I attended were the best resources for me. I really wanted to find someone to help who dealt with postpartum mood disorders.

I decided to do my own research on the Internet. I found a website called Pregnancy and Postpartum Support International (PPSI), www. postpartum.net, which led me to find a local postpartum support group.

I was ecstatic! It offered free child care, providing me much needed relief about what to do with my three young children.

The first day I attended the postpartum mood disorders group, I was the only one who showed up. This was a real bummer because I hoped to finally meet other women who had gone through similar experiences.

The support group was run by two older women: a nurse who dealt exclusively with postpartum mood disorders and a counselor. I had the entire two hours to share my story with them.

They told me that my story was dramatic, but that there are many other women like me out there who have suffered in similar ways. I found this hard to believe because I had never met anyone before with a story like mine.

Where are these other women? I desperately need to find them.

It was such a relief to know that I wasn't a total freak. Because I had been in a mental institution with people who were chronically ill, I assumed that's what I had become. When I learned that I would get over this and that there was help for my illness, I felt so much better.

I also had a few more medical professionals confirm that I was unlikely to have another episode unless I was to have another child. Since we aren't planning on having any more kids, I felt a sense of peace and relief.

The next week when I attended the support group, another woman was there named Beth. Her story was just as amazing as mine. She also had a traumatic birth story, led by weeks of suffering afterward. I finally felt a connection with someone.

Why couldn't anyone have connected me with these women earlier? This is exactly the type of support that I needed.

The support group led to a counselor, Crystal Clancy, a Licensed Marriage and Family Therapist. She had suffered from postpartum depression herself and has a specialization in perinatal mood disorders. Her office was located just minutes from my house, and I decided to give her a try.

Crystal was someone I felt an instant connection to. She could completely relate to my experience, unlike most of the providers I had recently encountered. She seemed like someone I could be friends with.

The room was warm and cozy. There was a children's play area, so it felt family-friendly. Crystal sat on a chair across from me rather than behind her desk, which made the session feel more conversational than therapist-to-patient. She also clearly explained what was going to happen in therapy, which made me relax.

Unlike the first therapist who tended to focus on extraneous events, Crystal made me think deeper about the situation than I ever had before.

I thanked God that I was finally getting the help I needed to recover. I began to have faith that I would get through this nightmare. I just wish I had found the right people sooner.

When I first saw Crystal, she was very concerned that I was still on such heavy-duty psychiatric drugs three months after my hospitalization. She said that I looked tired, spaced out, and could tell that I was heavily medicated.

One of her first missions was to see if my medications could be changed. During our second session we talked about my hospitalization, and she diagnosed me as having posttraumatic stress disorder (PTSD), a common condition after someone experiences a traumatic life event.

According to her checklist, I was experiencing the following PTSD symptoms:

- Witnessed trauma to self/others
- Fear / Helplessness / Horror response
- Breakdown / Panic
- Recurrent / Intrusive recalling of event
- Flashbacks when falling asleep every night
- Acting / Feeling as if event is recurring
- Distress at exposure to cues
- Physiological reactivity
- Anxiety
- Persistent increased arousal
- Irritability / Anger
- Hypervigilance

CHAPTER 22

C-Diff

I contracted a *can-be-fatal* disease called C-diff. Just what a person with panic disorder and PTSD needs!

Three weeks after my return home, my son Eithan was scheduled to have surgery. He was going to have a bronchoscopy and endoscopy to look for any anatomical defects that might be causing him to aspirate thin liquids. At the same time, he was going to have his adenoids removed to help his chronic sinusitis.

A few days before his surgery, I woke up feeling dizzy. I was scared that my anxiety was coming back. I was alone with the kids and they were just getting up. Every time I tried to walk, I felt like I would collapse.

I needed to call for help, but my cell phone was downstairs and we don't have a home phone. I asked four-year-old Evan to go downstairs and get my cell phone for me.

Eithan asked for breakfast, the baby cried, and Evan wondered what happened to me. Evan brought me the phone and I called my dad and asked him to come over right away and take care of the children. It took him about forty-five minutes to get to my house, and those were some of the most excruciating minutes ever.

I just lied in bed, leaving Evan to fend for himself and his brother and sister. I was completely worthless. Then it started and didn't stop for a week: *uncontrollable diarrhea.*

I couldn't even drink water; it would go right through me. After a few days of this I drove myself to an urgent care clinic. It was a Sunday morning and we were expecting company to come over and visit our new baby. I called our friends from the urgent care clinic to cancel plans once again.

The nurse sent me to the back room and started me on IV fluids. I was hooked to this machine but couldn't stay away from the bathroom. I must have gone in there at least thirty times in the two hours I was at the clinic. This was the worst physical sickness I had ever experienced. The doctor ran a number of tests on me and said they'd call me with the results in a few days.

A few days—I'm dying here!

They sent me home to rest. Yeah, good luck with that! I was a stay-at-home mom with a newborn and two toddlers. I knew I wouldn't be able to rest.

On Monday I went to my regular doctor's office, and they put me on another IV since I was severely dehydrated.

They asked me several questions about where I could have picked up this illness like, "Have you been to a foreign country?"

I told them I was recently hospitalized and they tested me for a bacterial infection called C. difficile (commonly called C-diff), which according to the Mayo Clinic, "C. difficile is a bacterium that can cause symptoms ranging from diarrhea to life-threatening inflammation of the colon. Illness from C. difficile most commonly affects older adults in hospitals or in long-term care facilities and typically occurs after use of antibiotic medications. C. difficile bacteria can be found throughout the environment—in soil, air, water, and human and animal feces."

Sure enough, that's what I had. As if the stress of being hospitalized for a mental illness wasn't bad enough, here was a nasty bacteria crawling inside me as a going-home present—most likely caused from coming in contact with my roommate's poop!

They also tested my potassium levels and discovered they were dangerously low, which probably caused my dizziness. I had to take huge banana-flavored horse pills and go in daily to the doctor's office to have my potassium levels monitored.

The next morning was Eithan's surgery. Before I had even gotten C-diff, we had agreed that I would stay home with Emily and Evan because watching my two-year-old son go through surgery in my vulnerable state would have been more than I could handle.

While Eithan was in surgery, my mom came over to help me with the two kids and give me some emotional support. I was still deathly sick with C-diff and went back to the clinic for a third round of IV fluids.

While I was sitting for a few hours at the clinic with my IV, my husband and I were texting back and forth giving each other updates about Eithan's surgery and my condition. This was not a good day! I did, however, remain amazingly calm. I think all I could do was worry about the next few minutes and try to make it through the moment.

Eithan was a real trooper and came through his surgery just fine. We were told it would take him a few days to recover, but he bounced back almost immediately.

We bought him a lifetime supply of popsicles, and he was a happy guy. His voice was a little scratchy, but that was all. He actually enjoyed the experience and took home several souvenirs from the hospital so he could play doctor.

Eirik even e-mailed me a picture of him in his tot-sized scrubs.

I worried that Eithan would get C-diff, but the doctor assured me that it was very unlikely I would pass it on to my family members. I did take extra precautions however, like spraying everything down with Lysol.

CHAPTER 23

Awakening

I lived life normally on the outside, but on the inside I still didn't feel like myself.

I was drowsy and spacey all of the time from the medication. My husband and I tried to get back our alone time that we usually have when the kids go to bed, but I would pass out on the couch by seven-thirty every night. I exerted every ounce of energy I had just taking care of the kids until he got home from work, and as soon as he walked in the door, I surrendered the kids to his care.

Looking after my three darlings seemed like an enormous task. I used to be a person who could juggle many things at once—I even thrived on it. But at this time in my life, I could barely muster up the energy to feed my children. There were many days that they wore their pajamas all day and went without their teeth brushed. I just did what I could to survive.

The littlest things would set me off. The startle reflex continued to haunt me. Whenever there was a slight noise out of context, I felt like something was crawling through my skin.

I felt depressed about not working and wished I hadn't quit my job. At least if I'd had that to go back to, maybe my life would seem more normal.

I would just stare at my three kids in amazement and wonder how I could care for them. It didn't seem possible.

My financial stress was relieved when I got a job teaching marketing online. But the stress of learning something new seemed like too much to handle. I was terrified that I wouldn't have the mental capacity to be able to handle the job, but I decided all I could do was try.

At the same time, a newspaper I had done freelance work for gave me an opportunity to write for them again, and I said yes. I didn't know how I was going to mentally pull it off, but I thought by getting these pieces of who I was back I'd start to feel like my old self again.

I don't know if this was a wise decision or not. On one hand, I had anxiety when my plate felt too full, but on the other hand I felt depressed being treated as a sick person who wasn't able to do anything mentally gratifying.

In January I took on a new marketing consulting client and had to write a marketing plan to present to their board of directors. It took me a lot longer than normal to write it, but I got it done. I was really nervous about taking on this project, but I felt very determined to prove to myself that I could do it. Once I finished the project, though it may not have been my greatest masterpiece, I felt very proud of how far I had come in my recovery.

We rescheduled Emily's baby-naming ceremony for February. I exchanged her original dress that was a size 0–3 months for one that was 3–6 months. The good news was it had gone on sale! The dress was hot pink, sleeveless with a velvet top and taffeta bottom. She also wore tiny newborn black patent shoes.

Everyone who was supposed to come to the first baby naming showed up. No one said a word about my condition. It was like there was this big elephant in the room that no one wanted to mention. I don't know if I would have said anything either if I was a guest at the party. After all, who wants to ruin a joyous occasion bringing up a very terrible time in our lives? Nonetheless, it would have been nice if someone asked how I was doing.

There is a real stigma about mental illness—one that I've always had too, that's why it was so difficult for me to accept my own diagnosis. I'm sure my friends and family were afraid to talk about my mental illness because it's a hard thing for most people to understand and accept.

Even though I wasn't fully recovered, I managed to seem enough like myself and had a great time. The food was beautiful. My mom and great-aunt Sophie made a delicious spread of desserts, fruits, and cake. The ceremony reminded me of how lucky I was to have such a beautiful family, and how far I had come.

I was finally feeling like the old me was starting to emerge, even if it wasn't all of the time. I became less worried about a relapse with each passing day.

Also that month, I met with a new psychiatrist at the same office where I saw Crystal Clancy. She was shocked that I was still taking the full load of meds from the hospital and made a plan to get me off of them as soon as possible.

At this time I experienced extreme fatigue, feeling on edge, had difficulty concentrating, and had gained a lot of weight. She assured me that I would feel better when we cut down on the medications. She was right and she was wrong.

Since I took such heavy-duty psychiatric drugs, there was a detoxing period that would take place. When I stopped taking Seroquel, one of the more potent drugs, I felt like I lost my mind. All of my senses were heightened. I was afraid of everything. But most of all, I was a Nervous Nelly. Everything made me nervous, even just talking to someone. I couldn't sit still for two seconds. Sitting for an hour talking to my counselor was extremely difficult.

During this detoxing period, I flew with my dad and son Evan to San Francisco to visit my brother and his family. Sitting still on the plane was torture. I wanted to bolt out of my seat. I didn't like feeling confined. I had a great time on the trip, but I was so anxious about everything.

The next morning after I flew home, I had an early morning appointment with the psychiatrist. I told her what was going on and that I was getting worse. She decided to increase my dosage of Lexapro, an antianxiety medicine, from twenty to thirty milligrams. She told me to stay off the Seroquel unless I felt I really needed it.

I can be kind of strong-willed, and I decided that no matter what I wasn't going to take any more Seroquel. I had had enough of that stuff! I didn't like feeling so heavily medicated.

Around this time, Eithan was diagnosed with kidney disease. It is the kind of mind-blowing news that no parent wants to hear—especially one who is recovering from a panic and anxiety disorder. However, I handled this news with relative ease, just as I normally would.

Of course I felt things that every mother would feel when her child is diagnosed with a serious illness—sadness, worry, and fear. But instead of these feelings consuming me, they stayed in check.

Eithan was put on a steroid medication for several months and recently went into remission. While there is an 80 percent chance of a recurrence, I feel prepared to deal with the situation.

Over the next several weeks, I slowly felt better. Then one day in March, six months after the birth of my daughter, I woke up and felt completely and 100 percent myself again (with a little help from Lexapro)!

It was the strangest awakening. I couldn't believe it! It was as if this other soul had left my body. It was at this point that I knew I had gotten through my crisis. I practically shouted it over the rooftops that I was recovered. I announced it to Eithan's early childhood class and told Regina immediately.

The nightmare was over, or so I thought.

CHAPTER 24

Discovery

After my *awakening* I thought I was fully recovered, end of story, but now I realize it was just the end of a chapter, and a new one is beginning.

Writing this book has been the most therapeutic thing I've ever done. I've learned more about myself and my condition than I ever thought possible. As the months have passed working on this book, it has been a never-ending journey of discovery and healing.

Until recently, I was convinced that I had never had any anxiety before the birth of Emily, but now I know it's been there for most of my adult life.

While I had always attributed the temporary paralysis after Eithan's birth to an epidural gone awry, I recently disvovered that this may actually have been a psychological, rather than neurological condition.

Regina had always been curious about this, as there was no logical medical diagnosis that could explain my symptoms. During my hospitalization, she mentioned this piece of my history to my psychiatrist, who agreed that this could easily meet the criteria for a classic conversion disorder, in which psychological symptoms manifest physically.

It has been a real awakening to discover that I had shown signs of postpartum anxiety with my second pregnancy, long before I recognized any of the symptoms.

I am so happy to have made this discovery, because one cannot heal unless you know what you are healing from. I am convinced I will become a much better version of myself through this process.

Since my awakening, I feel better than I have in my entire life. I am down to just one medication, Lexapro, an antianxiety medication. The fatigue that I experienced on Seroquel has gone away, and I don't feel drugged any more.

Life with my children is better than I could have ever imagined. I am enjoying being able to be there for them every day and seeing them grow. I cherish every moment with them more than I ever would have before. If I feel like I am having a bad day, I think about where I was and it puts my life into perspective.

My bond with Emily has become so strong that it is hard to imagine how I could have felt any resentment toward her, but mental illness does strange things to a person.

I look forward to rocking her to bed every night. Those quiet moments alone with my daughter are my greatest sense of joy.

It is unfortunate that I was robbed of those moments early on in her life, but it has made me appreciate them even more today. I just stare at her some days and admire what a beautiful little girl she is, and that I am so blessed to have her.

I have a new sense of calmness and peace in my life that I never felt before. Instead of feeling overwhelmed, I feel very capable of handling my three kids, the household, my part-time jobs, and my social life. For once, it all seems manageable and I have the sense of control I seem to need.

CHAPTER 25

Relapse

After a relaxing vacation in Myrtle Beach, I came home feeling like I drowned in a sea of chaos.

I started to become really overwhelmed at the ten loads of laundry that was piled up in front of me. I began thinking about all of the unfinished home improvement projects I had left behind.

While Eirik had the first day back off of work and was a huge help, I still felt like I had been hit by a tornado. All week I tried to unbury us from all of the packing and started going like the Energizer bunny. I just cleaned and cleaned and never stopped to take a breath.

I began to feel frantic and on edge all of the time. In addition, my social calendar was packed. I had plans every night—swimming lessons, girls' nights, and neighborhood barbecues.

About a week after our vacation and going on adrenaline all week, I had a Saturday home alone with Emily. Eirik and the boys were spending the day at Mall of America and I was hoping to get some work done around the house as well as socialize with the neighbors.

Several houses in our neighborhood had built a real eighteen-hole golf course, and every July they have a golf tournament. There are also several activities that take place throughout the weekend, such as a family breakfast, softball tournament, swimming, a barbecue, and a bonfire.

One of our neighbors, John, was divorcing and would be selling his house. We hoped to get a bigger house in the near future but weren't sure how we were going to pull it off because we owed more on our house than we could sell it for. Then I had this idea: *What if we buy John's house and he rents our house? Then everyone will be happy and life will be great.*

I became absolutely fixated on this idea to the point that I couldn't concentrate on anything else. I tried to grade papers for the marketing class I taught, but the papers just stared back at me. Emily took a nap, so I had a rare hour or so of time to myself.

I started researching the hell out of this idea. I went on the Internet and found John's house. I used a mortgage calculator to figure out the payments. It was Saturday, but I called several mortgage bankers to try and figure out if the transaction would work. I just kept getting voicemails which made me really agitated. Emily woke up, and I went to find John at the golf tournament. I hardly knew him, but I tracked him down and said, "We need to talk." He was busy running the golf tournament and was like, "Yeah, whatever."

The women were at John's house hanging out by the pool. I asked my friend Anne if John would mind if I looked at his house. I had never even been inside his house mind you, but I had already decided we *needed* to buy it.

Of course, Eirik knew nothing of this crazy idea. I looked through the house and it missed the one thing we were looking for—four bedrooms upstairs, the main reason we wanted a new house. Still, I didn't care. I was bound and determined to make this transaction work.

I went back to my house and called my realtor and told her all about my idea. I am sure she thought I was a little nutty as I told her Eirik didn't even know anything about this decision. I continued making phone calls and researching on the Internet all afternoon. I left Eirik several urgent messages. He didn't understand what was so urgent.

Later that evening, our whole family went to the barbecue. I watched John all night trying to find a good moment where I could slip in and tell him my great solution to both of our problems.

I finally came up to him and said, "I want to see your house. Actually, Anne showed it to me this afternoon. I think we need to buy it. I'll rent you my house. Do you want to come and look at it?"

Wow, when I read this now I realize how irrational I acted, and I am totally embarrassed by my behavior. He told me that he wasn't even sure that he could afford it because of the divorce and really had no interest in renting our house.

When we got home, I told Eirik all about my *brilliant* idea.

"We don't even know if this is the house we want," he said.

He seemed to stop me in my tracks.

The next day I spent most of the morning working on this book, and then I went to show the townhouse we own to a potential renter.

I was supposed to pick up Aunt Sophie and take her and the kids to my mom's house for dinner. The townhouse showing ran late, and I was rushing to get home to get the kids.

As I drove home I experienced another panic attack—the first one since my hospitalization nine months earlier. I felt shortness of breath, my chest was tight, and my adrenaline ran into overdrive. I knew it was a panic attack, and that made me panic even more!

After a lot of self-discovery during my recovery, I realized that I've had previous panic attacks, starting in my early twenties.

One happened when I was a communications assistant for a fast-food company right after I graduated college. I had come into conflict with my boss, and I was feeling like a real big failure. I couldn't breathe and began hyperventilating right there in the office.

The other time I can recall is a few years later, and I was also at work. Similarly, things weren't going well at work and I had feelings of inadequacy and failure. I started to get dizzy and faint. A friend drove me home from work early that day. I never sought medical attention or thought about it ever again.

In recent years, my obsessive tendencies have gotten worse. I will get an idea, such as we *need* to take a vacation, and I will stay up all night researching that idea, despite the fact that I have to wake up early the next day.

A friend described her alcoholic husband as "not having a shut-off valve." I realized that was the same thing I had, but my *drug* is my own head, not a substance. I've always thought this was a positive thing. "Look at me; I can accomplish so much in just one night!" Now I am realizing that this is a sickness.

I became more aware of my workaholic tendencies. While being productive is not necessarily a bad thing, I tend to take it to the excess. I get bored, then overschedule my life, do ten things at once most of the time, run on an adrenaline rush, then come crashing down with exhaustion.

Since I felt so great up until this point, when I had this latest breakdown, it made me realize how off the norm I really was. I had lived this way for so long that it seemed completely normal to me, though the people around me have noticed that I run around like a chicken with my head cut off most of the time.

Just when I thought that I was cured, I discovered that I have a long road of healing ahead of me. It's like peeling back layers of an onion. Once I think I've gotten a deep enough understanding of my illness, I discover a layer that goes even deeper.

Right now I am going back to my therapist, for what I'm sure will be a long time, to get the help I never knew I needed. While my anxiety may not be completely gone yet, I feel so empowered just by accepting it for what it is.

I am also experiencing frequent night terrors, a lingering effect from the posttraumatic stress disorder.

And to top it off, another new problem cropped up since my hospitalization—a phobia of used bandages.

I took my kids to the beach on my birthday this past summer, hoping for a fun and relaxing day. However, I felt like bandages were crawling out of the sand attacking me. I couldn't enjoy myself at all. I stood frozen in the sand and watched my kids play. All I wanted to do was run. We left early and I shook and trembled. We had gone to the same beach the year before and I didn't have any issues.

My therapist helped me discover that this is a symbolism for illness in my mind and a fear of getting sick and being hospitalized.

Eirik and I are attending some counseling sessions to learn how to deal with the aftermath of my illness and the abandonment he felt during that time.

I know that together, we will learn tools for how to cope and become a stronger family because of this difficult time we experienced.

CHAPTER 26

Healing

While the first few months of my daughter's life were a living hell, I feel that in a strange way it has helped me appreciate my children, my husband, and my life even more.

It's also given me a purpose. I want to be able to help other women who may be going through a similar experience and let them know that I understand.

I would love for there to be a place where new moms could go for support and healing, that is not in the confines of a mental health institution.

In the future I would love to see more education on postpartum anxiety and other perinatal mood disorders, not just depression.

As a survivor, I want to bring education to the forefront so other women can easily get the answers they are looking for.

I'd also like to see better transitional care from the hospital. A home health nurse would have allowed me to come home with my children a lot sooner and would have saved the insurance companies a lot of money since my hospitalization cost more than $1,000 a day.

I hope that with this book and by sharing my experience, I can give medical professionals better resources for their patients who are experiencing perinatal mood disorders, and let sufferers know that they aren't alone and that they will heal.

Thank you again to everyone who shared in my journey. You are the inspiration that gave this *Supermom* hope. I am learning to fly again. Each day is a new journey.

CHAPTER 27

Advice for Moms-to-Be and New Moms

While I'm not a medical professional, I have *lived* to tell my story about postpartum panic disorder. I have also met many wonderful survivors over the past year. From my own experience, postpartum support groups, survivor websites and blogs, medical professionals, and other women who have shared their stories, I want to give you some advice if you have just had a baby and are wondering if you may have a perinatal mood disorder.

First of all, you need to realize that perinatal mood disorders can happen to anyone, even if you've never had a prior history of mental illness or have had previous births that did not lead to any anxiety or depression.

"Postpartum mood disorders are very common, affecting 13.6 percent of new moms," said Wendy N. Davis, PhD, program director for Postpartum Support International (PSI).

Postpartum mood disorders can occur any time during the first year after birth, not just in the first few weeks, though sixty percent of women have onset during the first six weeks, according to PSI.

Every person, pregnancy, and situation is unique. Don't worry about the stigma of mental illness—getting help for yourself is the best thing that you can do for your family.

I was more worried about the label of being mentally ill than treating the problem. I had to overcome the shame of the disease and accept it for what it was in order to get the help I needed. Just because you have a postpartum mood disorder doesn't mean you're crazy.

The first question I had when I started getting anxiety symptoms was, "How could this happen to me?" I think postpartum anxiety issues stem from a strong cocktail of one part sleep deprivation; two parts of stress; one part of hormones gone awry; and three parts of being overwhelmed with responsibility.

To medicate or not? This has been a hot topic going around my survivor's group. I think that if you can get better using natural remedies, such as yoga, meditation, or positive affirmations that is the best way to go. Unfortunately for many of us, me included, our disease progressed too quickly and too severely to rely on natural remedies alone.

One thing I have learned about psychiatric medications is that they are not an exact science. Unfortunately, there is a lot of trial and error involved to see how the medications will react with your body's chemistry. It takes at least a few weeks for the medication to have its full effect.

While I was in the hospital, my medications were adjusted several times before they found the combination that worked best. While my stay at the hospital was traumatic and scary, I am glad that I was in a safe place while my body was adjusting to the meds, and that I could focus on myself and my recovery, not the needs of everyone else.

I have also learned that skipping doses of medication or weaning off of a medication can really mess you up. It takes a few weeks for your body to adjust to the change.

When I forgot my pills for two days, I hid myself in my bedroom and sobbed uncontrollably for no reason at all. This was a frightening experience but one that has taught me a lesson: *Don't forget to take your medicine!*

If your medicine isn't working for you, have yourself tested to make sure that you don't have a malabsorption problem to certain types of drugs. This has caused some women I know serious complications in their recovery from postpartum depression or anxiety.

Take care of yourself first and foremost after your delivery. Ask your partner, family, and friends for support. Don't worry about entertaining visitors. Your health needs to be a priority so you can take care of your baby. Accept help from anyone who is willing to offer it.

Sleep as much as you can. I think a lot of my problems were caused by severe sleep deprivation. Let the laundry pile up and feed the kids frozen pizza for a few weeks. Don't try to be a *Supermom* (look where it got me)!

Perinatal mood disorders can affect women in many different ways. Not everyone experiences crying jags or wanting to harm their baby. Be aware that any feelings that are out of the ordinary should be evaluated by a professional.

If you feel like something is wrong, it probably is. Only you know your body and your mind. Take this feeling seriously and get help right away. The quicker you can get help, the more likely you can prevent your disease from spiraling out of control. And if you are fine, no one will be upset with you if you don't have a postpartum mood disorder. It's better to be safe than sorry.

Don't suffer in silence. Make sure to tell someone that you need help and seek it immediately. Suffering alone can be deadly.

If you have unexplained physical symptoms, such as dizziness, loss of sensation, shakiness, or a tingling sensation, get checked out by a doctor immediately. If they can't find a medical diagnosis, realize that the symptoms may be mental and seek the help of a counselor or psychiatrist right away. Also, have your thyroid tested to rule out a physical problem.

Ninety-five percent of women with anxiety disorders are undiagnosed and untreated, according to experts at the *2010 Beyond the Baby Blues* conference in St. Paul, Minnesota.

Understand that people with Type A personalities are more prone to anxiety and panic disorders. If you are a *Supermom*, be especially aware of these disorders.

While you are pregnant, think of ways to change your lifestyle. Cut down on the number of extracurricular activities your kids are in and limit your social engagements to one per weekend so you can have some down time. These are rules that my husband has to constantly remind me to live with!

After the baby is born, don't plan to do anything except survive for the first few months. Wearing down your body can wear down your mind.

If you are feeling incapable of caring for yourself or your baby, admit yourself to a hospital or another safe place. While you will naturally feel guilty and a sense of abandonment, he or she will forgive you. Helping yourself is being the best mother you can be.

Realize that the road to recovery is a long one, but you will return to your old self with time and patience. I have found that there are several stages to perinatal mood disorders: symptoms, acceptance, rock bottom, a slow climb uphill, recovery, discovery, and lifestyle change.

Information is the key to understanding yourself. Try and gather as much information as you can about perinatal mood disorders while you are pregnant, rather than after you give birth when you may be in a more fragile state. The more you understand ahead of time, the better prepared you will be.

If you are suffering from a postpartum mood disorder, seek out others who have recovered. Never suffer in silence and never suffer alone. Realize that many other women have been where you are now and have gone on to be happy, content, and well-balanced mothers.

Most of all, have *hope*. In a time of great despair, this is the only thing that kept me going.

September 12, 2010

Dear Emily,

I can't believe in just a few short weeks we will be celebrating your first birthday. I am so proud to be your mommy. This birthday is extra special—it's a celebration of where we were and how far we've come.

When you are older, Em, I'll read you this book I wrote about what happened after your birth. I want you to know that I loved you from the day you were born, even when I was really sick, I always loved you and always will.

Your birth was not a mistake, it was the greatest blessing I could ever have wished for; it just didn't go as planned as I am learning, and you will too, that God often has his own plans for us.

You are the sweetest, funniest, and cutest little baby girl a mother could ask for. If there was such thing as perfection, you are it. Every time I look at you, I can't believe we created such a perfect baby. You are always happy, you make everyone laugh, and you are as beautiful as you are sweet.

My experience after your birth has taught me to cherish every moment that we have together. Every time I look at you, I appreciate you in a way that I might never have before. While it saddens me that we didn't bond at the beginning, I think we've more than made up for lost time over these last few months. And the good news is we have the rest of our lives together. There was a time when I wasn't sure I would get to raise you. Now I know we will be together forever.

I love you so much Emily Bemily Boo. I am so happy to be celebrating your first birthday with you. We made it! I can't wait to celebrate even more birthdays with you and watch you grow into a little girl, teenager, and a woman.

Happy birthday, Boo!

Love,

Mommy

To live is to suffer;
to survive is to find
some meaning in the
suffering.
                    —Friedrich Nietzsche

Remember, every
mom is a Super Mom.
Some bonds may
contain a weak link in
the beginning, but a
mother and child bond
can never be broken.

—Stacey

Glossary of Terms

affect. A subjective feeling or emotional tone often accompanied by bodily expressions noticeable to others

anxiety. An unpleasant feeling of fear and apprehension accompanied by increased psychological arousal; in learning theory, considered a drive that mediates between a threatening situation and avoidance behavior. Anxiety can be assessed by self-report, by measuring physiological arousal, and by observing overt behavior.

anxiety disorders. Disorders in which fear or tension is overriding and the primary disturbance including phobic disorders, panic disorder, generalized anxiety disorder, obsessive-compulsive disorder, acute stress disorder, and posttraumatic stress disorder.

compulsion. The irresistible urge to repeat an irrational act over and over again

conversion disorder. A somatoform disorder in which sensory or motor function are impaired, even though there is no detectable neurological explanation for the deficits.

depersonalization. An alteration in perception of the self in which the individual loses a sense of reality and feels estranged from the self and perhaps separated from the body; may be a temporary reaction to stress and fatigue or part of panic disorder, depersonalization disorder, or schizophrenia

derealization. Loss of the sense that the surroundings are real; present in several psychological disorders, such as panic disorder, depersonalization disorder, and schizophrenia

hallucinations. Perceptions in any sensory modality without relevant and adequate external stimuli

insight. An understanding of the motivational forces behind one's actions, thoughts, or behavior; self-knowledge.

lability. Emotional unstability

mood disorders. Disorders, such as depressive disorders or mania, in which there are disabling disturbances in emotion.

obsession. An intrusive or recurring thought that seems irrational and uncontrollable to the person experiencing it

panic attack. A sudden intense apprehension, terror, and impending doom, accompanied by symptoms, such as labored breathing, nausea, chest pain, feelings of choking or smothering, heart palpitations, dizziness, sweating, and trembling.

panic disorder. An anxiety disorder in which the individual has sudden inexplicable and frequent panic attacks, with or without agoraphobia.

posttraumatic stress disorder (PTSD). An anxiety disorder in which a particularly stressful event, such as military combat, rape, or a natural disaster, rings in its aftermath intrusive reexperiencing of the trauma, a numbing response to the outside world, estrangement from others, and a tendency to be easily startled as well as nightmares, recurrent dreams, and otherwise disturbed sleep.

psychosis. A severe mental illness in which thinking and emotion are so impaired that the individual is out of contact with reality

type A behavior pattern. One of two contrasting psychological patterns revealed through studies seeking the cause of coronary heart disease. Type A people are competitive, rushed, hostile, and overcommitted to their work, and are believed to be at heightened risk for heart disease; Type B people are more relaxed and relatively free of pressure.

Emergency Contacts

Immediate Emergency
911

National Suicide Prevention Lifeline
1-800-273-8255

Suicide Prevention Hotline
1-800-SUICIDE

National Postpartum Depression Hotline
1-800-PPD-MOMS

Postpartum Support International (PSI)
PPD Helpline: (not a twenty-four-hour hotline)
1-800-944-4773

Support Websites

Jenny's Light
Its mission is to improve and save lives by increasing awareness of all perinatal mood disorders including postpartum depression.
www.jennyslight.org

Mommies Cry Too
Mommies Cry Too is a peer-to-peer website created for and by postpartum sufferers and survivors.
www.mommiescrytoo.com

Postpartum Support International (PSI)
The purpose of the organization is to increase awareness among public and professional communities about the emotional changes that women

experience during pregnancy and postpartum.
http://postpartum.net

Depression After Delivery
This site has several links relevant to postpartum disorders and mental illnesses.
www.depressionafterdelivery.com

The National Institute of Mental Health
The National Institute of Mental Health (NIMH) is the largest scientific organization in the world dedicated to research focused on the understanding, treatment, and prevention of mental disorders and the promotion of mental health.
www.nimh.nih.gov

Online PPD Support Group
The purpose of this website is to offer information, support, and assistance to those dealing with postpartum mood disorders, their families, friends, physicians, and counselors.
www.ppdsupportpage.com

Pacific Post Partum Support Society
The Pacific Post Partum Support Society (PPPSS) is a nonprofit society which provides support to women and families experiencing depression or anxiety related to the birth or adoption of a baby.
www.postpartum.org

Postpartum Education for Parents
PEP (Postpartum Education for Parents), a group of trained parent volunteers, offers numerous programs to help parents and families thrive with their new children.
www.sbpep.org

The Postpartum Stress Center
The Postpartum Stress Center specializes in the diagnosis and treatment of prenatal and postpartum depression and anxiety disorders.
www.postpartumstress.com

US Department of Health and Human Services

Depression during and after pregnancy; a resource for women, their family and friends.
www.mchb.hrsa.gov/pregnancyandbeyond/depression/family.htm

PostpartumMen

PostpartumMen is a place for men with concerns about depression, anxiety, or other problems.
www.saddaddy.com

Postpartum Dads

Information for dads affected by perinatal mood disorders.
www.postpartumdads.org

Postpartum Progress

National blog promoting progress in treatment and comfort among sufferers of postpartum mood disorders. Postpartum Support International free phone support chats each Wednesday for moms and the first Monday of every month for dads. These sessions provide a free forum for information, support, and connection.
www.postpartum.net

Recommended Reading

Bennett, Shoshana S., and Pec Indman. *Beyond the Blues: A Guide to Understanding and Treating Prenatal and Postpartum Depression.* San Jose, CA: Moodswings Press, 2003.

Kleinman, Karen, and Valerie D. Raskin, MD. *This Isn't What I Expected: Overcoming Postpartum Depression.* New York: Bantam Books, 1994.

Mauthner, Natasha S. *The Darkest Days of My Life: Stories of Postpartum Depression.* Cambridge, MA: Harvard University Press, 2002.

Nordstrom, Kelly. *Unperfect: A Not-So-Graceful Journey into Motherhood.* The Woodlands, TX: Indigo Heart Publishing, 2010.

Pedersen, Julie. *The Panic Diaries: The Frightful, Sometimes Hilarious Truths About Panic Attacks.* Berkeley, CA: Ulysses Press, 2004.

Sebastian, Linda. *Overcoming Postpartum Depression and Anxiety.* Omaha, NE: Addicus Books, 1998.

Shields, Brooke. *Down Came the Rain: My Journey Through Postpartum Depression.* New York, NY: Hyperion Books, 2005.

Twomey, Theresa. *Understanding Postpartum Psychosis: A Temporary Madness.* Westport, CT: Praeger Publishers, 2009.

Wiegartz, Pamela. *The Pregnancy and Postpartum Anxiety Workbook: Practical Skills to Help You Overcome Anxiety, Worry, Panic Attacks, Obsessions, and Compulsions.* Oakland, CA: New Harbinger Publications, Inc., 2009.